CELTIC

myths

Steve Eddy
and
Claire Hamilton

TEACH YOURSELF BOOKS

For UK order queries: please contact Bookpoint Ltd, 130 Milton Park, Abingdon, Oxon OX14 4SB. Telephone: (44) 01235 827720. Fax: (44) 01235 400454. Lines are open from 9.00–18.00, Monday to Saturday, with a 24-hour message answering service. Email address: orders@bookpoint.co.uk

For U.S.A. order queries: please contact McGraw-Hill Customer Services, P.O. Box 545, Blacklick, OH 43004-0545, U.S.A. Telephone: 1-800-722-4726. Fax: 1-614-755-5645.

For Canada order queries: please contact McGraw-Hill Ryerson Ltd., 300 Water St, Whitby, Ontario L1N 9B6, Canada. Telephone: 905 430 5000. Fax: 905 430 5020.

Long renowned as the authoritative source for self-guided learning – with more than 30 million copies sold worldwide – the *Teach Yourself* series includes over 300 titles in the fields of languages, crafts, hobbies, business and education.

British Library Cataloguing in Publication Data
A catalogue record for this title is available from The British Library.

Library of Congress Catalog Card Number: On file

First published in UK 2001 by Hodder Headline Plc, 338 Euston Road, London, NW1 3BH.

First published in US 2001 by Contemporary Books, A Division of The McGraw-Hill Companies, 4255 West Touhy Avenue, Lincolnwood (Chicago), Illinois 60712–1975 U.S.A.

The 'Teach Yourself' name and logo are registered trade marks of Hodder & Stoughton Ltd.

Typeset by Transet Limited, Coventry, England.
Printed in Great Britain for Hodder & Stoughton Educational, a division of Hodder Headline Plc, 338 Euston Road, London NW1 3BH by Cox & Wyman Ltd, Reading, Berkshire.

Impression number   10 9 8 7 6 5 4 3 2 1
Year   2007 2006 2005 2004 2003 2002 2001

CONTENTS

INTRODUCTION

A vital factor in the development of the human race has been its use of symbols to represent ideas or urges that cannot easily be defined. A symbol can magically bring an idea to life by appealing to the creative power of the imagination. It can also offer several layers of meaning in a single image. For example when Theseus tracks down the Minotaur in the Cretan labyrinth, he lays down a thread to guide his return. This may symbolize divine inspiration, or the link between the conscious mind and the unconscious. The labyrinth itself can be seen as a symbol of the individual's tortuous journey to self-knowledge and of the mysteries of the feminine.

Myths, then, are symbolic stories. They have evolved through oral tradition and they have guided, inspired and psychically nourished humanity for thousands of years.

Myths interpreted

Mythology has been used by poets, playwrights and artists for centuries. The nineteenth century, however, saw the rise of scientific rationalism and of social realism in the arts. Myths were in danger of being demoted to the status of quaint old stories about non-existent gods. A 'myth' began to mean simply a widely held but mistaken belief.

With the rise of psychology, however, myths found a new status – although there was controversy about their origins and functions. Freud saw them as expressing repressed impulses commonly found in the personal unconscious. The myth of Oedipus, for example, expressed a boy's socially unacceptable desire to kill his father and sleep with his mother.

Claude Levi-Strauss saw myths as stemming from a human need to make sense of the world. By this model, the myths worldwide in which human beings are fashioned from clay by a divine potter, such as the Egyptian Ptah, fulfil our need to know how and why we came to be here. Other widespread myths explain death and the seasons.

Another view focuses on myth as magic. Stories of hero gods descending into the Underworld in the west and emerging in the east reflect the setting and rising of the sun. Myths in which an ageing goddess is reborn as a youthful virgin reflect the return of spring after winter. This kind of myth must have reassured early man. More important, it is likely that the repeated telling of stories symbolizing the rising of the sun, the return of spring or the ripening of crops was a magical way of making these things happen.

Many commentators have noted the similarities between myths in different cultures. One theory is that this can be explained by migration, trade contact and the exchange of myths between conquerors and conquered. There is certainly some truth in this, for example in the interweaving of Aztec and Mayan myths. However, this can hardly explain similarities such as the appearance of 'Trickster' gods: the infant Hermes stealing Apollo's cattle, the Norse Loki cutting off the golden tresses of Thor's wife, Sif, or a similarly mischievous deity of the North American Winnebago Indians.

Jung and the theory of archetypes

The exploration of myths found a new dimension in the work of Carl Jung. Whereas Freud saw the unconscious as being entirely personal, the product of a lifetime's repressed sexual urges, Jung identified a layer of consciousness below this – the collective unconscious. This is a vast psychic pool of energized symbols shared by humanity as a whole. It is filled with 'archetypes': symbolic figures, such as the Trickster just mentioned, the Mother and the Father. They also include the animus and anima, which are the undeveloped and largely unacknowledged opposite sex parts of, respectively, the female and male psyche. Another important archetype is the Shadow, which embodies all that we deny in ourselves and 'project' onto people we dislike. These archetypes form the *dramatis personae* of myth. Thus myths offer a way for cultures to explore their collective impulses and to express them creatively, rather than harmfully.

Myths, dreams and the individual

Jung recognized dreams as doorways between an individual and the collective unconscious. Many dreams, he said, expressed archetypes that might otherwise be projected onto the waking world as irrational fears, delusions or hatreds. Joseph Campbell, who has developed this idea, writes: 'Here we can begin to see a way of working with myths on a personal level, for our own development.' Campbell and other writers have also pointed out that myths are still emerging and developing in the present day. On the social level we see this in the recurrence of mythical archetypes in popular culture, for example in the hugely successful *Star Wars* films.

Jung saw myths as representing the individual's journey towards psychic wholeness. The aim of this book is not only to show the power of myth to entertain and enrich on a narrative level, but also to facilitate this journey. It retells the myths and explores the interpretations – cultural, moral, psychological and spiritual – to which they lend themselves. It also shows how the themes of Celtic myths echo those of other cultures worldwide, in a way that argues a fundamental psychic content common to all humanity.

Celtic pronunciation guide

Spellings used in this book are derived from the original Celtic language. For Welsh this is actually a better pronunciation guide, since there is often no English equivalent for a Welsh sound (as in the softly guttural *ll* sound, whose nearest equivalent is *cl* or *chl*). In the phonetic approximations here, *dh* is pronounced *th* as in 'then'; *ch* is guttural, not hard as in 'cheese'; *gh* is softly guttural.

Aengus	Angus
Ailill	Alil
Amargin	Avar*gh*in

Annwn	Anoon
Badb	Ba*dh*v
Blodeuwedd	Blod-eye-we*dh*
Brug	Brew
Caoilte	Kweeltya
Cathbad	Kathva*dh*
Conchobor	Kon-*ch*-ovor
Cuchulainn	Ku-*ch*ull-in
Dahut	Da-hoot
Deichtine	De*ch*-tin-e
Diarmuid	Dermot
Dyfed	Duvv-ed (as in 'dove')
Emain Macha	Evin Ma-*ch*a
Emer	Ay-ver
Eoghan	Yo-*gh*-an
Finn (Fionn) mac Cumhail	Fyun m' Cool
Gronwy Pebyr	Gronwy Pevyr
Penllyn	Pen-*ch*lin
Gradh	Grave
Grainne	Graun-yeh
Gwynedd	Gweh-ne*dh*
Laeg	Loy*gh*
Lleu Llaw Gyffes	*Ch*lay Chlow Geh-feth
Lugh	Loo
Lughaid	Lewey
Macha	Ma-*ch*a
Medb	Ma*dh*v or Mave
Naoise	Noy-shee
Niamh	Neem
Oisin	Osheen
Pwll	Poo*ch*l – with *oo* as in 'f*oo*t'
Scathach	Scaw-tha*ch*
Tain Bo Cuailnge	Toyn Bo Cooling
Usna	Oozna (with *oo* as in 'f*oo*t')
Ys	Ees
Ysbaddaden	Ehs-ba*dh*-adn

1 | CELTIC CULTURE

Prior to Roman or Christian influence the Celts were not literate. Their myths were passed on orally, largely in poetic form by bards, until the coming of Christianity in the fifth century onwards. It was the monks, many of whom had been born into pagan families, who wrote down the myths and it is thanks to them that so many survive today.

One might expect Christian monks to have qualms about recording pagan tales, especially given the laborious nature of the work, but this does not seem to have been the case. St Patrick, who brought Christianity to Ireland in 432, is said to have had his doubts about the old stories until he received a vision in which he was told to respect and record them. Some of the myths have been Christianized, especially those recorded in Wales. However, a particular feature of Celtic myths may have prevented this from happening more often: namely, the way in which deities have been euhemerized (given human form), so that, unlike the Greek myths, they are not obviously of a religious nature. It is tempting to think that some early converts, such as St Columbus, whose bardic training influenced his Christianity, actually encouraged an encodification of druidic beliefs in the apparently innocent stories.

Who were the Celts?

The Celts probably began to emerge as a distinctive culture in central Europe during the second millennium BCE. One of the earliest references to them is by the Greek historian Herodotus (fifth century BCE), who refers to them as the *Keltoi*. Aggressive, creative and full of energy, they spread in all directions, to Galatia in Asia Minor, to western Greece, westwards to Galicia in north-west Spain, Britain and Ireland – and even, according to recent burial excavations, to western China. Celtic armies sacked Rome in 390 BCE and Delphi in 279 BCE.

However, we should guard against thinking of these early Celts as a single people. They thought of themselves primarily as members of their own tribe and although several tribes could unite to confront a common enemy – notably Rome – they were just as likely to be fighting each other. In north-west Europe there were two broad groups of Celts defined by language. Those in Britain (later just in Wales and Cornwall) and in Brittany were Brythonic; those in Scotland, Ireland and the Isle of Man were Goidelic. But what they all shared was a recognizably homogeneous culture. This included their basic character, outlook and values, their religious beliefs and gods, a family of languages and an inheritance of related myths.

Character, outlook and values

Our written accounts of the Celts come from classical writers, who were often impressed by their civilized ways. In the fifth century BCE Helicanos of Lesbos described their sense of justice, which is also attested to by records of sophisticated legal systems. In the myths, too, there is a strong sense of correct behaviour, fair play and reparation. Conchobor loses the support of Fergus by betraying the Sons of Usna (see pages 42–5); Gilvaethwy is turned into a succession of animals for raping Goewin (see page 66); and Pwll has to compensate Arawn for setting his hounds on the other man's stag.

Linked to this sense of justice is a sense of personal pride and honour. This is always present in the conduct of Cuchulainn and the other warriors in the *Tain Bo Cuailnge*, as it is in Homer's *Iliad*. Cuchulainn almost always keeps his word. Honour appears in a different form in Pwll's keeping of his promise to Arawn and in his noble refusal to take advantage of Arawn's wife.

The Celts also prided themselves on their bravery and martial skill. Although lacking the discipline and strategy of the Romans, they were valued as passionate fighters and many became mercenaries in armies as far afield as Egypt. The Romanized Greek geographer Strabo called them 'war-mad' (4.4.1–2), which could certainly describe Celtic heroes such as Cuchulainn, who seem to live for the glory of combat. Neither was this renowned courage and fierceness limited to the men. Marcellinus writes of the Gallic Celts:

> A whole band of foreigners will be unable to cope with one of them in a fight, if he call in his wife, stronger than he by far and with flashing eyes; least of all when she swells her neck and gnashes her teeth, and poising her huge white arms, proceeds to rain punches mingled with kicks, like shots discharged by the twisted cords of a catapult. (XV.12.2)

This is reflected in the myths, which are full of strong women.

Besides this prowess in battle, the Celts were notable orators and had a high regard for truth, seeing it as the foundation of the word, and of speech. They loved poetry and according to Julius Caesar a Celtic bard might spend 20 years memorizing the full collection of verses. Hence in the myths there is oratory on the battlefield and when Gwydion charms the transformed and near-dead Lleu out of an oak tree, it is with *englyns* – magical verses (see page 83). There is even a Celtic god of eloquence, Oghma, who gave his name to a druidic alphabet, *ogham* (pronounced *oe-m*), used for magical inscriptions and possibly as a kind of shorthand. Oghma's Gallic equivalent, Ogmios, was depicted with chains running from his tongue to human beings, showing his power over them.

At the same time the Celts loved to play with words. Diodorus Siculus writes: 'In conversation they use few words and speak in riddles, for the most part hinting at things and leaving a great deal to be understood.' Riddles, which are a particular form of magical truth-telling, therefore play a part in such myths as 'Diarmuid and Grainne'. They also used the power of the word in magical incantation, as does Gwydion, but it could also be used in a very different way, by the satirist. In the *Tain* the hero Ferdia agrees to fight his old friend Cuchulainn only when Medb threatens to subject him to the terrible shame of being satirized. According to an early Irish story the Formorian king Bres was obliged to abdicate when the druid Coirpre satirized him and brought him out in boils.

Religious beliefs

Roman writers described the Celts as being superstitious, but this really points to their having beliefs that the logically minded Romans did not understand. The spiritual mentors of the Celts were the druids, who according to classical writers had great knowledge of philosophy, magic, science and astronomy. They were a priestly order, and yet they could marry and were often fighting men – as was Calatin, whose daughters prove to be Cuchulainn's nemesis. They played a magical role in some battles, as they do in the last great battle of the *Tain*. However, unlike other men, they were not obliged to fight and, in fact, druids of opposing tribes would sometimes meet together to try to resolve the conflict – or else try to influence the battle by magic.

The power of the druid features in many Celtic myths. One example is 'The Voyage of Maeldun' (see page 97): Maeldun becomes fated to go off on his long and dangerous sea adventure when he breaks the prescription of a druid who has told him exactly how many men to take with him. Yet the voyage itself can be interpreted as a druidic initiation. Another mythical episode in which a druid plays a key part is when Cuchulainn overhears the druid Cathbad predicting the fate of any youth who takes up arms on that day (see page 23). This points to a central Celtic belief – namely that each day had a particular quality that would influence the outcome of enterprises begun on that day. Archaeologically this is backed up by the Coligny calendar (first century BCE), now in the Palais des Arts, Lyon. Among other things, it designates some days *mat* (good) and others *anm* (not good).

The Celts also believed in reincarnation. Seeing time as cyclical, they considered human life to be a perpetual alternation between this world and the Otherworld – sometimes referred to as the Land of Youth, or Tir na n'Og. This was another world existing parallel to this one. It was sometimes thought to be in the west – where the sun sets, but in Irish myths it is sometimes accessed through fairy mounds, the *sidhe*. When Pwll first sees the fairy woman Rhiannon he is sitting on a fairy mound at Arberth. The Otherworld was both the land to which one's spirit went after death, prior to reincarnation, and a land to which the living might go. However, just as few Greek heroes manage to visit Hades and return, few mythical Celts return from the Otherworld except by reincarnation. Cuchulainn is an exception. He develops a wasting sickness and eventually learns that he can be cured of this in the Otherworld, and that a fairy woman, Fann is in love with him. He enjoys the love of Fann, and the splendours of the Otherworld, for a time, but is then fetched back by his wife Emer. Even then, he has to be given a drink of forgetfulness to stop him going mad with longing for Fann.

Celtic gods and goddesses

In Celtic myths the gods appear as recognizable deities less often than one might expect. This is partly because, as noted earlier, they have been euhemerized, especially in the later Irish myths and in all the Welsh ones. We can see this clearly in the case of the god Lugh, who gives his name to the Irish summer festival of Lughnasadh. In the earliest Irish myths – in the Mythical History and Ulster Cycles – he is clearly a deity. In the former cycle he offers himself as the saviour of the Tuatha dé Danann, the predecessors of the Milesians or Gaels. Seeking entry at the palace of King Nuada of the Silver Hand, at Tara, he announces each of his skills in turn – 'Blacksmith, warrior, musician, poet, scholar ...' and each time is refused entry, until he points out that no one else combines all these skills in one person, as he does. In the Ulster Cycle Lugh becomes the father of Cuchulainn by transforming himself into a tiny worm which Cuchulainn's mother then drinks in her wine. In the *Mabinogion*, the main source of British myths, Lugh has become the much more human Lleu Llaw Gyfes, nephew (and possibly son) of the magician Gwydion. He is skilled and protected by charms, but he is not obviously a god: in fact, he almost dies.

Lugh shares some characteristics with the Dagda, a larger-than-life figure prominent in myths of the Tuatha dé Danann. Like Lugh, he is powerful and omnicompetent. Yet he is often represented as a rather comic figure whose short tunic fails to cover his buttocks and whose huge club has to be carried on wheels. He has great magical powers and he possesses a harp which comes to him when he calls and a cauldron of abundance which restores dead warriors to life (but without powers of speech, perhaps in case they say too much about the afterlife). This cauldron, or one like it, is pictured on the Gundestrup cauldron, found in Denmark. Cauldrons are a common symbol of abundance and rebirth in Celtic myths. In another form, the goblet, it occurs in the story of Cuchulainn's conception.

Another significant god, although he appears less often in the myths, is Cernunnos. Lord of the animals, and of 'the Wild Hunt', he is usually shown wearing a stag's antlers. This indeed is the form in which he appears on the Gundestrup cauldron. Since he is also connected to the Underworld and fertility, he may be linked to Arawn, Lord of Annwn, who first appears to the hero Pwll as a huntsman (see page 112).

More significant in the later myths is the Irish and Scottish Angus (Oenghus) Og, the 'Young Son', linked to the British Mabon. Son of the Dagda and Boann, the river goddess, he was associated with youth, beauty and charm, but he is particularly a god of love. He is the lover of Caer, the Swan Maiden, and turns himself into a swan in order to woo her – reminiscent of Zeus with Leda. Angus helps Midhir to marry Etain and he hides the lovers Diarmuid (Angus' foster-son) and Grainne from the pursuing Finn (see page 54).

Powerful though these gods were, the Celtic goddesses were perhaps even more so. They were closely associated with the land and in this identification they sometimes seem to be aspects of a single all-embracing Goddess. Their link to the seasonal cycles, to fertility and death may partly account for the fact that a single goddess often takes three forms or aspects – usually maiden, mother and crone. Thus the Irish Eriu is also Fodla and Banbha. The pantheon of Irish gods is said to come from the Tuatha dé Danann, the children of the goddess Danu, whose British equivalent is Don. Macha, who gives her name to the Ulster capital of Emain Macha, is a euhemerized mother goddesss associated with horses, because when pregnant she is forced to run a race against a king's chariot. She gives birth to twins but dies pronouncing a curse on the men of Ulster: for nine generations, whenever they are in their hour of greatest need, they will suffer the pangs of childbirth for five days and four nights. Only Cuchulainn was exempt.

Celtic goddesses could be life-giving and sustaining, but were also, in their dark aspect, associated with sex and death, which in Celtic terms are part of the round of life. The most powerful Irish example is the red-haired shape-shifting Morrigan, said to have coupled with the Dagda. In the *Tain* she offers Cuchulainn her favours and becomes his enemy when he rejects her. When he dies, she perches triumphantly on his shoulder in the form of a crow or raven. She is triple-aspected with Nemhain and Badb. The British equivalent of the Morrigan is Ceridwen, who pursues Gwion Bach through various shape-shifts until she finally gobbles him up as a hen and eventually gives birth to him as the bard Taliesin.

Geasa – the magical prohibition

The Celts had a strong sense of fate, and linked to this is the peculiarly Celtic concept of *geis* (plural *geasa*). This is not a 'taboo', because it applies to an individual, not (in the myths at least) to a whole tribe. Moreover, there is the implication that sooner or later it will be broken, with fatal consequences. It is impossible to say how *geasa* come about. Sometimes a woman with magical powers puts a hero 'under *geis*', obliging him to do as she says. Deirdre does this to Naoise, and Grainne does it to Diarmuid. A druid can also put someone under *geis*. In some cases the *geis* is connected to an incident, as in the case of Cuchulainn, who as a child kills a guard dog and takes its place for a year. We find later in his life that he is under *geis* never to eat dog meat, but no direct link between the incident and the *geis* is made.

Some commentators have related *geisa* to animal totemism: an individual has a vision of an animal, which gives him power – but which he will lose by eating or hunting that animal. Something similar applied in Native American tribes. Diarmuid is under *geis* never to hunt boar, and dies when tricked into doing so. However, not all *geasa* involve animals: Diarmuid is also under *geis* never to leave a palace by a wicket gate. All we can say, ultimately, is that a *geis* is a magical prohibition, particularly applying to heroes and kings, whose death will eventually come by their being somehow made to break it.

The sources of the myths

The surviving Celtic myths come from Scotland and Ireland, which were at one time closely related, from Wales (although many of these originated orally further east) and from Brittany. No myths survive from Romanized areas, such as Gaul on the Continent. They do not appear to have been written down in Latin.

The greatest body of myth comes from Ireland, which was untouched by the Romans, although much of its mythic material was destroyed by indiscriminate Viking marauders. The myths are divided into four groups:

1 The Mythical Invasions Cycle, featuring the successive waves of races populating Ireland: the Partholonians, the Nemedians, the Firbolgs, the Tuatha dé Danann and finally the Milesians, or Gaels. All four groups had to contend with a race of malevolent giants, the Formorians.

2 The Ulster Cycle, which includes the epic the *Tain Bo Cuailnge*.

3 The Fenian (Ossian) Cycle, centring on Finn mac Cumhail, leader of the *Fianna*, the élite warrior band, and his son Oisin.

4 The Immrama, comprising wonder voyages such as 'The Voyage of Maeldun'.

A major Irish source is the *Lebor na hUidre* (the Book of the Dun Cow), written down in the seventh century on the hide of a cow owned by St Ciaran. The surviving copy was compiled in Clonmacnoise Monastery by Maelmuiri, a monk killed by Vikings in 1106. The *Tain Bo Cuailnge* (Cattle Raid of Cooley) appears, though mutilated, in the Book of the Dun Cow. This 'Celtic *Iliad*' focuses on Queen Medb's determination to capture the Brown Bull of Ulster, in order to match the White Bull of Connacht, owned by her husband Ailill. Later Irish sources for the *Tain*, and other stories, are the Yellow Book of Lecan (in Trinity College, Dublin) and the Book of Leinster, both fourteenth century. *The Colloquy of the Ancients*, an extended conversation between Patrick, Oisin and Caoilte, was transcribed in the sixteenth-century Book of the Dean of Lismore.

All the Welsh myths in this volume come from the *Mabinogion*, the group of early Welsh tales collected in the White Book of Rhydderch (*c.* 1325). A more complete collection is contained in the Red Book of Hergest (*c.* 1400). The Welsh tales are more corrupted than the Irish ones, having been first recorded at a later date, in a Norman-ruled Christian society. They show considerable Christian and French courtly influence and have suffered from being copied inexpertly and from the copyist filling in the gaps from his imagination. The *Mabinogion* is divided into four branches and a further seven tales.

The myths of Brittany have suffered most, owing to the French government's efforts to eradicate the Breton language and culture in the interests of nationalism. Despite this, many Christianized myths found their way into Albert Legrand's anthology of saints' lives (1636). More often referred to is the *Barzaz Breiz*, or Songs of Brittany, collected from living folk memory by Viscount Hersart de la Villemarque in 1838. Since Breton myths had continued to evolve up to that time, they contain few of the martial elements found in the Ulster Cycle and the saints make frequent appearances. Nevertheless they are a vital part of the Celtic heritage and show an interesting blend of pagan and Christian elements.

2 | THE HARP OF THE DAGDA

This story concerns the most ancient Irish Celtic gods, the first generation of the Tuatha dé Danann who had to fight off the giant races of the Firbolgs and the Formorians. Their history is found in the *Lebor Gabála*, 'The Book of Invasions'.

When the fairy race of the Tuatha dé Danann arrived in Ireland, they came like a mist across the waters, bringing with them magical gifts. These were the *lia fail* – the coronation stone, the spear of Lugh, the sword of Nuada and the great cauldron of the Dagda, which was said to be able to restore life.

The Dagda himself was known as the Good God and he was chief of the gods at this time. Besides his cauldron, he had a harp which was battle-scarred and made of oak. It was covered in rich decorations including a double-headed fish which ran up and down the curved pillar and had jewels for its eyes. Although he had a harper, Uaithne, he could also play it himself.

The Dagda had this harp with him always – he even took it into battle. So it was, that after the second Battle of *Mag Tuiread*, or Moytura, the Dagda discovered that his harp, together with his harper, had been captured by the Formorians and taken with them in their flight. Angered beyond measure, he set out with his son Aengus Og to reclaim it.

Stealthily they approached the Formorian camp. Soon they could hear the sounds of the feasting hall in which Bres, the Formorian king, was dining. Approaching the doorway, they could just make out through the smoke and candle flame the outline of the old harp hanging on the wall. Then the Dagda entered boldly and summoned his harp with this chant:

Come *Daurdabla*, apple-sweet murmurer
Come, *Coir-cethair-chuir*, four-angled frame of harmony,
Come summer, come winter,
Out of the mouths of harps and bags and pipes!

Immediately the old harp flew to his hand across the hall, killing nine men as it came. A shocked hush fell on the company. In the silence the Dagda laid his hands on the strings and unleashed the Three Noble Strains of Ireland that he had bound into his harp. First, he played the *goltrai*, or strain of weeping, so that all present began to mourn and lament their defeat. Then he played the *geantrai*, the strain of merriment, so that the company turned to laughter and drunken foolery. Lastly, he played the *suantrai*, or sleep-strain, whereupon the warriors fell into a profound slumber. After this the Dagda and Aengus Og left the camp as quietly as they had come, taking Uaithne and the harp with them.

The 'Brian Boru' harp in Trinity College Library, Dublin

COMMENTARY

The Tuatha dé Danann

The Tuatha dé Danann were the children of the great goddess Dana. They are depicted as magical fairy people who were later overrun by the Milesians who allowed them to reside underground in the *sidhe*, or fairy mounds. They were traditionally believed to have arrived like a mist, but this is a poetic reflection of the fact that they ritually burned their boats on landing in Ireland so that they could never leave.

The Dagda

The Dagda was the chief of the Tuatha but, because he is coarser than their other gods, he might be a remnant of a much older deity. His antiquity is demonstrated by the fact that he carried a great club. At the same time, like Lugh, he claimed to be multi-skilled. This is indicated by his name, the Good God: to the Celts, 'good' meant skilled and the Dagda is depicted as being a master of music along with a range of other magical and warrior attributes. He also had a prodigious appetite and earlier in the Battle of Moytura was forced by the Formorians to eat a huge amount of porridge which had been prepared in his own cauldron. Undaunted, he ate the lot, after which his stomach was so distended that his tunic no longer covered it.

The Dagda can be seen as an ancient father-god who was symbolically linked to the great mother goddess through his great cauldron of regeneration. (The Dagda's cauldron became a forerunner of the Arthurian Holy Grail.) Being multi-skilled, he also demonstrates the Celtic understanding that gods were not limited to a single skill or attribute.

The Three Noble Strains

These relate to the three sons that Uaithne, the Dagda's harper, fathered on the Goddess Boann. She gave birth to the oldest, *Goltraiges*, in great pain, to the second, *Gentraiges*, in joy, while, after the third one, *Suantres*, she became heavy with fatigue. All three were harpers and became representative of the three main effects, or strains, of music.

The power of music

Music was of great importance to the Celts because they believed it had the power to enchant. The names of the Three Noble Strains end in *trai*, which means enchanter. Music could therefore magically summon or control emotion. It could also take the hearer into a place of dream and vision or bring the soothing of forgetfulness. It was an integral part of the Otherworld. The sound of beautiful music greeted the entry of every hero into this realm, often being produced by magical birds. Magical birds also attended the silver-stringed harp of Aengus Og who used it, like Apollo, to charm them. For the harp was considered particularly magical. It was often owned and played by gods. It was the favoured accompaniment for telling the old tales, being able to conjure all the different moods as well as to accompany the vocal declamations of poetry. Thus every bard was expected to be skilled on it. Later, broken-stringed, the harp came to symbolize the sorrows of Ireland. Its magical music also retreated, along with the Tuatha, into the *sidhe*. Some evocative Irish music today is said to have come from tunes overheard in fairy revels.

3 THE BIRTH AND BOYHOOD OF CUCHULAINN

Cuchulainn is the hero of the Ulster Cycle of myths known as the Red Branch. The story of his birth is told in the Book of the Dun Cow. That of his boyhood deeds, including how he earned his name, is related by Fergus mac Roth in the *Tain Bo Cuailnge*. The *Tain* also appears in the Book of the Dun Cow. The version of the boyhood deeds given here comes largely from this source and from the Yellow Book of Lecan, supplemented by a more recent version of the *Tain* found in the Book of Leinster.

In written form the Cuchulainn myth dates at least from the eighth century, although the verse passages are older. In oral form the stories probably date from at least the first century BCE, judging by the battle tactics used, notably chariot fighting. They show little sign of being Christianized: in the whole course of his myth, Cuchulainn shows remorse for his slaughters only twice – when he unwittingly kills his own son and when he is obliged to fight and kill his close friend Ferdia.

Conchobor and his nobles were at Emain Macha one winter's day when a huge flock of birds approached. They were beautiful, but they settled on the land and ate up all the plants and grass – even the roots, so that the land was laid waste. Conchobor and the men of Ulster set out to hunt them, the king taking as his charioteer his sister Deichtine. There were nine flights of birds, each numbering a score. A silver chain linked each pair of birds, and each flight was led by a silver-yoked pair.

The Ulstermen pursued the birds to Brug on the River Boyne, and as night fell, accompanied by a heavy snowfall, they took shelter in a humble house. The man of the house welcomed them in, but warned them that his pregnant wife had just gone into labour. Deichtine went in to the woman and helped her to bear a son and at that same moment a mare outside the house gave birth to two foals. The Ulstermen took charge of the boy and gave him the foals for a present. Deichtine, for her part, was immediately enamoured of the boy and agreed to become his foster-mother.

In the morning the birds had disappeared. More strange than this, the house and its occupants had also disappeared without trace.

There are those who say the boy with the mysterious parents was Cuchulainn. Others say that this boy died and that Deichtine's grief was great at the loss of her foster-son. When she asked for a drink, a tiny creature found its way into the goblet and entered her. That night she dreamed of the god Lugh, the son of Light. He told her that the boy she had fostered was his and that now she would bear him a son, who was to be called Setanta.

Deichtine grew big with child, and since no one knew who the father was it was rumoured that Conchobor himself had made his sister pregnant in his drunkenness. Now a child must have a father and so Conchobor gave Deichtine to a noble, Sualdam mac Roic, in marriage. However, being ashamed to go pregnant to her marriage bed, Deichtine lost the baby. In time, she became pregnant again. She gave birth to a son and called him Setanta – although the whole of Ireland was later to know him by a different name.

A dispute now arose about who should rear the boy. Another sister of Conchobor, Finnchaem, said that it should be she, as she was already full of love for him. Then Sencha said that his own prowess and wisdom fitted him for the job; Blai Briuga insisted that he would be best able to provide for the boy; Fergus the King's messenger argued for his own strength, skill, rank and riches; and the druid and poet-prince Amargin reminded them all of his eloquence and broadness of mind. Conchobor therefore decided to leave the decision to the judge Morann – who in due course ruled that the boy should be raised by all four men, with Finnchaem providing 'the teats of a mother'. In addition Conchobor himself took the boy as his foster-son.

Cuchulainn was raised in the south of Ulster on Murtheimne Plain. At an early age he heard tales of the exploits of the boys of Emain and decided he wanted to join them.

'Not until there are some Ulster warriors to go with you', said his mother.

'That's too long to wait,' protested the boy. 'Tell me the way and I'll go alone.'

'It's a hard road,' said his mother.

'Nevertheless, I'll try it.'

Off went the boy, armed with a toy shield and javelin and carrying his hurley stick and ball. The way was hard, over bleak mountains and peat bogs, but the boy made rapid progress, throwing his javelin ahead of him and catching it before it could touch the ground.

Soon he came to Emain, where he came across the boy troop playing hurley. He ran up to them without getting them to pledge his safety – which was the normal course of action with these boys. Taking this as a challenge, they shouted at the intruder and then sent their javelins flying at him. There were three times 50 boys, but to their surprise he fended off all their javelins on his little wooden shield. Then they hurled their hurley balls at him, but he stopped them all on his chest and continued to advance. With only their hurley sticks left, the boys aimed these at the newcomer, but he evaded them all – except for a few that for his own amusement he plucked out of the air as they whistled overhead.

Now, for the first time in his life, the boy was possessed by a battle fury that was to become the terror of armies in years to come – his Warp-Spasm. The hairs on his head stood up like nails hammered in, with a tongue of flame on each one. One eye became narrower than that of a needle and sank so far into his head that not even a crane could reach it; the other grew and bulged like a goblet. He bared his teeth from ear to ear and peeled back his lips to reveal his gullet. His calves and thigh muscles spun back to front and a hero's halo rose up from the top of his head. In this awesome form he launched himself on the astonished boy troop, most of whom fled before him, through the gates of Emain, where King Conchobor sat playing the board-game *fidchell* with Fergus.

'These boys are receiving rough treatment,' said Conchobor, grabbing the pursuing newcomer by the wrist as he leapt over the *fidchell* board.

'No more than they deserve,' protested the boy. 'I came to join their game and they treated me roughly.'

'Whose son are you?' asked Conchobor.

'I am Setanta, son of Sualdam and your own sister Deichtine. I didn't expect to come under attack here.'

'You should have put yourself under the boys' protection, but now I place you under mine,' said Conchobor. 'Where are you going now?'

'To offer the boys my protection.'

Conchobor made the boy promise this and soon the boys that were struck down were being helped up and treated for their injuries.

On another occasion, when Setanta, as he was still known, was six years old, he was playing ball against the whole of the boy troop. King Conchobor was about to set off to be feasted by Culann the Smith. As was his custom before setting out, he called at the hurley field to watch the boys and to receive their blessing. Now he was amazed to see one boy beating all the rest – at Shoot-the-Goal, at wrestling and at the Stripping-Game, in which he stripped them all naked while they could not remove so much as the brooch from his cloak.

'Come, lad, and be a guest at the feast to which I am going,' said Conchobor. Far from being afraid to turn down a King's invitation, the boy answered that he had not yet had his fill of play, and would follow on later. Some of the boy troop groaned in disappointment.

Conchobor set off towards the feast. As Culann was not a particularly wealthy man, Conchobor was considerately taking only 50 chariots of his greatest champions with him to the feast – the élite of Ulster. Conchobor and the 50 chariots arrived, to be greeted by the strong-armed smith.

'Is that all of you?' asked Culann. 'Or are you expecting anyone else? I have a guard-dog, the most ferocious hound that ever lived and if you're all here, I'll set him loose to guard the house and cattle.'

Forgetting his invitation to the boy-hero, Conchobor agreed to this and settled down to enjoy the feast with his men.

Meanwhile, Setanta had taken his fill of play, leaving the boy troop too exhausted to carry on anyway. Still full of life himself, he played as he went, tossing up his ball, then aiming the stick to hit it, then launching the javelin after them both and catching it before it struck the ground. He came to Culann's enclosure and continued to advance towards the house. The huge hound smelled and heard him coming, bayed once and then charged snarling and slavering towards the boy.

Setanta, never varying the rhythm of his game, watched the fast-approaching hound. Then, at the last moment, he hurled his ball with such force into the animal's open jaws that it shot down the throat of the unfortunate creature and disembowelled it. Hearing the sound of savagery outside, Conchobor remembered his arrangement with the boy and was struck with anguish. The men of Ulster rushed outside as fast as they could, but little hoping to find the boy alive. When they did, they gave a shout of joy and carried the boy in to the grateful king.

Culann approached slowly, like a man pulled in two directions. 'You are welcome, boy, for your mother's sake,' he said. 'But for my own part it was a bad day when I decided to give this feast, for without my hound I am ruined and my household is a desert. That hound protected and guarded our herds, our possessions and our honour.'

Brightly the boy replied, 'No matter. I'll rear a pup from the same parentage and train him to guard you well. Until that pup is ready, I'll be your hound and guard you and your estate – and the whole of Murtheimne Plain.'

At this the Druid Cathbad spoke up. 'You shall be called Cuchulainn – the Hound of Culann.'

Cuchulainn was pleased at this. And for ever after, that was his name, and he defended the whole of Ulster.

COMMENTARY

In Cuchulainn's birth and boyhood we see several attributes shared by mythical heroes in many cultures as they start out on their difficult and fated journeys through life. It is typical of the hero archetype that Cuchulainn has a mysterious and wonderful birth and that he is associated from the first with the great and good, in this case the King of Ulster and his sister. There are many heroes in myth and legend who have illustrious beginnings. In some cases this simply reflects the overall grandeur of their lives, but in Cuchulainn's it provides him with the best possible training to nurture his special talents to perfection and it helps to give him a special obligation to protect Ulster.

The triple birth

At a first reading, the story, with its three separate conceptions, two actual births and two deaths, could seem to be a confused merging of several different versions. We might take the first two conceptions, with the boy who dies and the one who is stillborn, as dress rehearsals for the actual birth of the hero. However, if we take the story as complex rather than confused, it takes on a new meaning. Although the first boy dies and the second is stillborn, they are all part of the hero's birth story – aspects of a single birth and the fact that they are presented as a single story underpins this.

First, we have the omens that something remarkable is about to take place – like the star in Christ's nativity story. In this case we have Conchobor, with Deichtine and the men of Ulster, hunting the great flock of birds. They ride out in nine chariots and there are nine flights of birds. The number nine might, of course, be associated with the nine months of pregnancy, but it was also magical to the Celts, since it is three times three – the Celts being fond of presenting things (especially deities) as triple-aspected. Birds themselves are symbols of the soul and of the Otherworld and were used in druidic divination. The silver chains between the pairs could point to marital ties, but, more esoterically, they suggest the tie between the soul and the body.

The birds lead the royal hunting party to Brug na Boyne, which is on the very borders of Conchobor's territory – symbolically on the edge of consciousness. It is also a place with spiritual significance for the Irish Celts, the site of the great burial mound of Newgrange, where the sun is reborn at dawn on the winter solstice, as its rays penetrate to the womb of the earth and linger for a few minutes on a stone altar at the end of a long passage. In addition the falling snow purifies the landscape by blotting out the ordinary world.

At this point the story takes on a notable feature found in another tradition of hero myths: the hero with apparently humble origins. The Christ story is an obvious example of this. Perceval in the Arthurian tradition is another. The implication is that the hero's lowly circumstances conceal supernatural parentage or blessings. Conchobor's party is obliged to take shelter in what seems to be a poor man's house. Its disappearance in the morning is a sure sign that the couple were supernatural beings. Here then, in this first birth, we see Cuchulainn's parentage as wholly spiritual or Otherworldly.

The birth of the foals at the same moment as the boy links them to him. In addition the fact that they are given to him and then later go on to become Cuchulainn's chariot horses (see Chapter 4, 'The Death of Cuchulainn'), further identifies this first boy with Cuchulainn. The horses can also be seen as an aspect of Cuchulainn's nature. Note, too, that the baby and foals are born at night, which for the Celts was the start of the daily cycle.

The second baby, conceived after Deichtine dreams of the god Lugh (Light), has one supernatural parent and one human one. The way in which she is impregnated is interesting. The goblet is a miniature version of the cauldron of regeneration possessed by the Dagda (see page 13), which points to the Celtic belief in reincarnation. The tiny thing or worm (depending on the version) represents the germ of life, although at another level it may relate to the biblical Holy Spirit.

Finally, losing this child, Deichtine has a third child, this time with a human father. However, Cuchulainn's powers are superhuman, godlike. So Cuchulainn is a being whose birth into this world of matter has occurred in three stages of descent from the world of spirit. Yet the births are essentially part of a process of incarnation.

The fostering

It was customary for the Celtic nobility to foster their children out, possibly to cement extended family ties and prevent feuding, so Cuchulainn's fostering is not significant in itself. However, the fact that notable people vie for the honour is unusual. On one level the outcome – that he gets the benefits of all six parents (five fathers and a mother, in addition to his real mother) – just means that his talents are excellently nurtured. However, there is another possible interpretation. If Cuchulainn, like other heroes, is linked to the Sun, then his foster-mother could represent the Moon, and the five foster-fathers the five planets known to the Celts, together with the attributes or powers associated with them.

Setting out

Like other heroes, Cuchulainn displays great prowess from an early age. In Greek myth, Heracles and Theseus show similar early promise. Cuchulainn is to have a short life, and he has to cram a lot into it, so it is no wonder that at the age of five he decides to go on the initial (and initiatory) journey on which so many fledgling heroes embark. Many do so on reaching puberty, but Cuchulainn is precocious. Naturally he decides to go the difficult way, over the mountains. This is reminiscent of Theseus, who opts for the dangerous overland route to Athens rather than the safer and shorter sea voyage. Theseus is setting out to find his father, and in a sense Cuchulainn is doing the same. Conchobor may actually be his real father (incest notwithstanding), is certainly his foster-father (and a king) and features far more in the young hero's subsequent story than does Sualdam.

In making this journey and finding this father-figure Cuchulainn is undergoing his first initiation on the road to becoming a man. Psychologically, he is abandoning the safety of the mother for the uncertainty of the confrontation with the father. Spiritually, he is leaving behind the comfort of the familiar for the quest for his true self.

The boy troop

Arriving at the court of Conchobor with his toy spear and toy shield, Cuchulainn has something of the innocent about him. He is unaware of the rules of this unfamiliar place, but since he is a hero in the making, he merely overrides them with his own prowess. The Warp-Spasm is like an extreme form of the Viking berserker's wild fury. Yet it is more than this: Cuchulainn is a godlike figure and here we see him – not for the last time – as the archetype of the Destroyer god, a Celtic Shiva whose power is terrifying yet awe-inspiring.

The hound of Culann

Next we have the episode in which the young boy, still called Setanta, earns his new name. In his desire to continue his play, rather than go straight to the feast, we see a child behaving naturally, yet in his ability to beat the entire boy troop single-handed we see a godlike figure. In Conchobor's forgotten invitation we see a certain paternal neglect with which heroes often have to contend. At the same time, this turns out to be another initiation. Cuchulainn has to cross a threshold guarded, as thresholds often are, by a fearsome hound – like Cerberus the three-headed guard-dog of the Greek Hades. He passes this test by remaining completely cool in the face of its savage fury, confident in his own skills and unafraid of death – and perhaps at this point not even aware of it.

The boy shows his mettle by defeating the beast and his nobility by taking its place. The Celts associated dogs with loyalty and with healing, although many cultures (such as the Egyptian) associate them with death owing to their habit of scavenging. Cuchulainn is certainly loyal in his defence of Ulster. There is also a hint of totemism here. Cuchulainn becomes identified with the dog and it becomes one of his *geasa* never to eat dog meat. This is to have fatal consequences, as the next story relates.

4 THE DEATH OF CUCHULAINN

The background to the death of this Irish hero lies in the *Tain Bo Cuailnge*, in which Cuchulainn makes an enemy of Queen Medb, but the story of Cuchulainn's death is told in the Book of Leinster. Later versions may reflect earlier versions since lost.

From his earliest years Cuchulainn made a point of giving way to no man, never accepting defeat, and never turning away from an honourable fight. As a boy he tricked his foster-father, King Conchobor, into arming him on a day when the druid Cathbad had predicted that whoever took up arms on that day would have a glorious but short life. Later, a similar fate was predicted for the young hero by Scathach, the warrior druidess to whom he was sent for training in the arts of war. Chanting in a clairvoyant trance, the *imbas forosnai*, she foretold his great deeds and untimely death.

As a youth Cuchulainn played a major part in defending Ulster from King Ailill and Queen Medb of Connacht when they mounted their attempt to carry off the Brown Bull of Ulster. He slew Connacht heroes by the hundreds, until he agreed to leave Medb's forces in peace at night and meet their greatest fighters in single combat at a ford on the River Cronn. He was unaided by the other Ulstermen, who were suffering at that time from a protracted bout of the birth pangs inflicted on them by the curse of Macha.

After nearly dying of wounds received in the terrible fight with his old friend Ferdia, Cuchulainn was finally relieved by the men of Ulster and lived to recover and return to his home on the Plain of Murtheimne. However, by this time he had made many enemies. There was hardly a man in Ireland who had not lost a relative to him. And Queen Medb, a powerful woman and a warrior in her own right, would not be quick to forget her humiliation at his hands.

Now among those who had come against Cuchulainn at the ford was a druid called Calatin, who had attacked Cuchulainn with his twenty sons, claiming that this was fair single combat as all the sons came of a single father, himself. Cuchulainn had killed them all, but Calatin's wife had already been pregnant. When she bore three daughters, Medb decided to make them the instruments of her revenge.

Medb took the baby girls and cruelly mutilated them, cutting off their right legs and left arms, so that they would be bitter, and better fitted for the task for which she intended them. She cultivated in them a single-minded hatred for the Hound of Ulster, the cause of their being without father or brother, and when they were old enough she sent them out into the world to acquire a thorough knowledge of the black arts. Thus they became adept in the most malevolent skills of druidism and witchcraft and they returned to Medb burning with a desire to use them against the man who had killed their father and brothers, Cuchulainn.

Medb now gathered together another great army and especially sought the support of two men ill disposed towards Cuchulainn – Lughaid and Erc, who had both lost fathers to Cuchulainn. Medb's army descended on Ulster during the time of the Ulstermen's pangs and began to plunder and burn a swathe across the land. Conchobor quickly guessed that the real object of the expedition was the life of Cuchulainn, and he lost no time in sending his messenger, the woman Lavarcam, to persuade Cuchulainn to leave his home on the Plain of Muirtheimne and come to Emain to be under the King's protection.

When Lavarcam found Cuchulainn, upon the seashore, he was aiming slingshots at the seabirds. They flew overhead in great numbers, yet the man who normally aimed with such delicate precision that he could stun a bird and restore it to life, then stun it again, and who never missed his target, found that today he could hit not one bird. This seemed to him a very bad omen, and so it was with reluctance that he left his home and accompanied Conchobor's messenger to Emain.

At Emain, Conchobor ordered poets, musicians and men of knowledge to entertain and occupy the hero, and Cuchulainn's loving wife Emer led the many women who attempted to distract him from the thought of the approaching army of Connacht. Meanwhile Medb's army advanced and razed Dundealgan, Cuchulainn's home, to the ground.

As for the three daughters of Calatin, they began to practise their evil arts. Out of the soil, and the oak leaves and burs, they conjured an illusory battle, in which battalions of men clashed and the air was fraught with the sound of desperate conflict. Cuchulainn looked out upon the sight of battle and his ears were filled with the fury of it. It took all the powers of the old Druid Cathbad to restrain him from rushing out to defend the apparently beleaguered city.

However, even Cathbad could not prevent Cuchulainn from looking, and there the Hound of Ulster thought he saw Gradh, son of Lir, amidst the throng, and he thought he heard the son of Mangur playing sweet strains of the harp to inspire the army. Now Cuchulainn knew that to see and hear these things was forbidden him by *geis*, and so he knew that the saving strength of his virtue was undermined by the daughter of Calatin and that his promised end was approaching.

Then one of the daughters of Calatin took the form of a crow and flew around him taunting him with jibes to defend his people if he were indeed a man. Cuchulainn knew that the battle was one of enchantment and illusion, yet it was torment to him to see and hear it and yet do nothing. And all the while the sound of the harp played upon his senses and upon his mind so that he was deeply troubled.

Cathbad assured him that if he could only resist the enchantments for three days, then they would have no more power and he would be free of them. That night the women and druids attending Cuchulainn decided to lead him away to a valley so remote that it was called Deaf Valley, so that he would be deaf to the terrible enchantments.

The daughters of Calatin were at a loss when they looked for Cuchulainn the next day, but guessing that he had been hidden away, they rose up on a breath of enchantment, like buzzards riding a March wind and they soared over the whole province hunting the Hound of Ulster. At length they spotted his grey war-horse, the Liath Macha, guarding the way into the valley and so they began their enchantments again. But although Cuchulainn was not deaf to the din of battle, the women of Ulster succeeded in quieting him and persuading him to ignore the noise.

When Cuchulainn failed to appear, the daughters of Calatin realized that their ruse had failed. Furious, and risking all on a last attempt, one of the daughters thrust her way right into the fortress where Cuchulainn was being entertained. Changing her appearance to that of a waiting woman, she persuaded Cuchulainn's mistress Niamh and the other women to step outside. As soon as they did, she raised a magical fog that prevented them from finding their way back in. None could be sure which way to go and great was their distress that Cuchulainn might be in danger without them.

Next the artful daughter exchanged her own misshapen appearance for that of the fair-faced Niamh. Finding Cuchulainn she softly berated him: 'Rise up, Cuchulainn! Take up your javelin and defend your people or all your honour will be as dust in the wind.'

Cuchulainn was amazed, because Niamh had made him promise not to take up arms without her leave and he thought she would not grant that until the danger to his life had passed. 'Since it is you who says it, Niamh,' Cuchulainn said, 'I will go. But after this I will not trust to women, as I thought you would never allow me for all the world's gold.' He rose, saying to himself, 'I have no further reason to protect my life, for my time has come and all my *geasa* are broken. Niamh herself has let me go, and so I shall.'

As he strode out of the fortress, the real Niamh, finding her way through the thinning fog, flung herself at him in desperation. 'Cuchulainn, it was not me who gave you leave. You were tricked by a daughter of Calatin. Return, I entreat you.' But her tears and pleadings failed to move him and he commanded Laeg, his charioteer, to catch his horses and yoke them for battle.

As Cuchulainn went out it seemed to him that he saw the whole of Conchobor's city overthrown and burning, the enemy despoiling the city in whatever way they pleased, and Emer's own house cast over the ramparts and all of Emain a seething mass of smoke, flames and destruction.

As Cuchulainn went, other ill omens occurred. His brooch fell and pierced his foot, drawing blood. His war-horse refused to be harnessed, except at Cuchulainn's own persuasion and even then the beast wept tears of blood. Then when he had passed the plain of Mogna, he came upon three hags huddled round a fire. They were roasting poisoned dog's flesh on holly spits. One of the hags turned a leering face to him.

'Come, Cuchulainn, sit and eat with us.'

'I shall not,' answered Cuchulainn, for it was a *geis* to him to eat dog – his own namesake.

The hags, knowing that it was another *geis* for him to refuse food offered at a cooking fire, taunted him for scorning their humble hospitality and again invited him to join them. Caught between two *geasa*, Cuchulainn reluctantly accepted a half of the dog that one of the hags gave him with her left hand. He took it with his left hand and ate, and when he placed part of the meat under his left thigh the whole of his left side was cursed and became weak. The three hags, the daughters of Calatin – for so they were – laughed grimly, for they saw their revenge in sight.

Leaving the hags and riding on, Cuchulainn met Medb's army on the plain of Muirtheimne, his own home ground. Although weakened, he displayed his thunder feats from the back of his chariot and he showed them all the feats of a warrior. His onslaught upon the enemy was fierce. The heads that he broke and the red bones he scattered were as plentiful as the grains of sand in the sea, the bright stars in the dark sky and the oak leaves in the forest. The whole plain became grey with the brains of his enemies.

The scheme devised by Erc, one of Cuchulainn's foremost enemies, was that two pairs of men should pretend to fight at each end of the army and that in each case a druid should ask Cuchulainn to separate the men and should then ask for his spear. This plan was put into action, but Cuchulainn separated the men by killing them, and each time reversed his spear and with its butt killed the druid. The first spear was picked up by Lughaid, who hurled it, killing Cuchulainn's charioteer, the ever-faithful Laeg. The second spear was picked up by Erc, who cast it at Cuchulainn's noble war-horse, the Liath Macha. Cuchulainn fondly bid the animal farewell and it galloped off to its place of origin, a mountain lake in Armagh.

**The death of Cuchulain: based on a bronze statue by
Oliver Shepherd, 1916, in Dublin Main Post Office**

Cuchulainn aimed the butt of his spear at a third druid and this time
it was retrieved by Lughaid, who hurled it with all the might that
his breeding and bitterness gave him and pierced the noble flesh of
Cuchulainn, wounding him mortally. At the same time
Cuchulainn's other horse, the Black of Saingliu, broke loose and
galloped off to its lake-deep home in Munster. Cuchulainn lay
dying in his chariot. Raising himself with great effort, he staggered
to a lake nearby, where he drank and washed off his blood, holding
his guts in with one hand.

Then Cuchulainn focused his blurring vision on a tall white pillar of stone close to the lake and made painfully towards it, limping across the rough ground. Reaching it at last, he unfastened his girdle and looped it around the pillar and around himself, so that he was held upright, with his sword still clasped in his right hand. Although he knew he was fading fast, his last wish was to die on his feet.

The men of Connacht began to approach Cuchulainn, but suddenly there was a drumming on the turf and Cuchulainn's horse the Liath Macha was among them, nostrils flaring, hooves flying, sinking his teeth into any man who dared come near to Cuchulainn. And at last Badb, sister of the Morrigan, and goddess of death in battle, came in the shape of a raven and alighted on Cuchulainn's shoulder, and the men of Connacht knew that he was dead.

Lughaid now approached. Searching for signs of life and finding none, he lifted up Cuchulainn's drooping head by the hair and with one stroke severed it from his body.

Great was the weeping of Emer and Niamh and of all the women of Ulster for Cuchulainn. The men fell silent in sorrow, for they knew that his like would not be seen among them again.

COMMENTARY

A fated life

Like other heroes, Cuchulainn has a fated life. But, as a hero, he actively chooses his fate and from there on he is strongly marked for an early death, like a sacrificial lamb. He overhears a druid saying that any young man who takes arms on this day will have a short but glorious life and that, of course, is what Cuchulainn wants. Like Homer's heroes, he prefers glory to long life. However, although the Greeks of the *Iliad* were in some ways more sophisticated than their Celtic contemporaries, Cuchulainn does have a strong sense of service to his people, which may be a development of the hero ideal from that of mere personal glorification. True, he wants personal glory, as did all Celtic warriors. But an important aspect of this is that the glory is earned in protecting Ulster and by self-sacrifice. The fatedness of Cuchulainn's death is later reinforced by Scathach's prediction.

The Celtic belief that each day would produce its own particular fruit was one shared by other cultures, including that of the Greeks. The mother of Alexander the Great held back her labour in order to give birth to Alexander at the best moment for a great hero to be born. Also common to most cultures is the belief that omens were indications of fate and just as Cuchulainn's birth was presaged by mysterious birds, so birds – or Cuchulainn's inability to hit them – presage his demise.

Enemies

Powerful people often make powerful enemies, and not least in myths. Take for example Heracles, relentlessly pursued by the goddess Hera, and Odysseus, persecuted by Poseidon. In the case of Cuchulainn, his enemies bring about his downfall. Although Cuchulainn is said to be loved by many women, his two strongest enemies are both female. The first, Medb, is mortal – although she can also be seen as a goddess figure. The second, the Morrigan, is the dark goddess, the goddess as crone. In the *Tain Bo Cuailnge* Cuchulainn offends her by refusing her offer of love when she comes to him as a princess when he is preoccupied with fighting single combats with the heroes of Connacht. His rejection of her could be seen as a form of *hubris*, the particular pride that makes heroes set themselves on a level with the gods. It could also be seen as a rejection of the feminine. In some versions of the story it is the Morrigan, not Badb, who perches triumphantly on Cuchulainn's shoulder at the moment of his death, and in some sources these goddesses seem to be one.

The three daughters of Calatin are also powerful enemies, although at first driven on by Medb. Indistinguishable from each other, they represent another triplicity, something like the Witches in Shakespeare's *Macbeth*. Lughaid and Erc, Cuchulainn's main male enemies, are really instruments of the more powerful female figures.

Protectors

Cuchulainn, however, also has female protectors. They join with the druids to keep him from acting on the enchantments of the daughters of Calatin. Foremost among them is his wife Emer, who elsewhere shows her courage and determination by going into the Otherworld, armed, at the head of a troop of women, to wrest her husband back from the bewitching fairy woman Fann. Then there is Niamh, Cuchulainn's lover, who seems equally anxious to save him. We could see these women as representing a feminine, nurturing force in the universe, or even Cuchulainn's own instinct for self-preservation.

Battling with illusion

The illusory battle conjured up by the daughters of Calatin is reminiscent of Buddhist visions of the world by which all worldly phenomena are seen as illusory – the works of Mara. Conflict and destruction, as Joseph Campbell has pointed out, are undesirable only on the dualistic, conditioned level at which we habitually live. At a higher level they represent the interplay of balanced forces. The illusion arises only from our limited perspective. In Hindu terms, Vishnu the Preserver and Shiva the Destroyer are one god.

There is something Otherworldly both in the distracting harp-playing that Cuchulainn hears and in the Valley of the Deaf into which he is taken. This valley represents another consciousness and his horse stands guard like a sentinel on the edge of dreams. The valley, too, represents the Otherworld, a world beyond this life, one in which Cuchulainn is safe. When the daughters of Calatin discover his whereabouts, they have found their way deeper into his mind. The fog, too, is Otherworldly, and it joins with the daughters' shape-shifting to confuse Cuchulainn and create a mood of uncertainty. What we assume to be the real world is, in the end, only our own perception of that world. When Cuchulainn goes out to the battle, he is doing what we all must do: acting on the available evidence. And in acting for the right reasons, even if mistakenly, he is heroic. He is also choosing to return to the hurly-burly of life, to do his duty rather than staying safe in the Valley of the Deaf.

Defeated by treachery

The fact that Cuchulainn is tricked into breaking his *geasa* is important. As a hero, a shining example, he has to be defeated by trickery and treachery, not by any weakness of his own. In Shakespeare, we see something similar in Macbeth's defeat by the Witches' equivocation, although Macbeth's own failings contribute to his downfall. Cuchulainn, however, as a more archetypal hero, has no personal weaknesses.

Cuchulainn becomes physically weakened when he breaks his *geis* not to eat dog meat. He loses much of the strength of his left side, relating to the right brain. He retains his left-brain willpower intact. It is of course impressive that despite being weakened he wreaks havoc on the field of battle, and even that he continues to observe the rules, handing over the spears butt first to the druids – even if so forcibly as to kill them!

Cuchulainn's faithful charioteer Laeg is killed before Cuchulainn himself, signifying the loss of an aspect of Cuchulainn's personality: the practical helper, who controls and guides Cuchulainn's physical vehicle – literally his chariot. Then his horses – animal aspects of himself – are mortally wounded. Note that these horses by some accounts are the foals presented to the hero as a baby (see page 15), while in the one used here they come from lakes. Finally, Cuchulainn himself is pierced by Lughaid's spear, with Erc lurking nearby. Cuchulainn drags himself to a lake – a symbol of the unconscious and of the waters of life, washing and purifying himself. Then with supreme willpower he hauls himself to the pillar of stone. In one view he is motivated, still, by desire for glory – wanting to die standing up; in another he is taking this combined symbol of earth and phallic masculinity as his support, binding himself to the world for a few moments longer, asserting life in death. The image of his doomed determination has been used in a striking statue in the Dublin Post Office, commemorating Irish resistance to English rule in the 1916 Easter Rising.

5 | FINN AND THE SALMON OF WISDOM

This Irish story from the boyhood of Finn mac Cumhail was originally written in a little tract on a fragment of the ninth-century Psalter of Cashel. It is translated in Volume IV of the *Transactions of the Ossianic Society*.

An old druid, Finn the Seer, sat by a deep pool, called Fec's Pool, on the banks of the river Boyne. For seven years he sat there while the wily old river shivered and wrinkled its surface like an old snakeskin, scribbling out the same patterns that can be found carved on the great entrance stones of the old tomb chambers of Howth and Nowth and Newgrange.

But it was not the insistent scribbling of the waters of the Boyne that held Finn's attention; he was staring at the surface of Fec's deep pool, maddened by the crimson-red bubbles that continually rose and burst over it.

The pool itself was fringed with nine hazel trees which were constantly dropping beautiful crimson hazelnuts into the water. And it was these nuts, filled with the essence of all that is most bewitching and inspiring in literature and poetry, that kept bursting their richness and staining the surface of the water.

Now Finn the Seer knew that deep in the murky depths of the pool, so deep that they almost touched the origins and springs of the world itself, lurked five large, sleek salmon. The old Seer had never so much as glimpsed them, but had heard tell that when they cavorted and twisted around in the water, the underside of their bellies could be seen speckled with shimmery crimson-red stains. This was because whenever the hazelnuts fell into the water the salmon darted forward to eat them. For this reason they were known as the five sacred Salmon of Wisdom or Inspiration.

Finn the Seer had spent a lifetime studying the arts of poesie, prophesy, augury and other forms of divination. It had been revealed to him by Otherworldly powers that one named Finn was destined to catch and eat one of the Salmon of Wisdom and that, having eaten of it, he would become imbued with special knowledge and achieve great deeds. And Finn the Seer could be forgiven for thinking, or even hoping against hope, that it was he himself who was chosen for such a glorious destiny. So, for seven years he had sat by the pool, waiting to catch one of the magical Salmon.

Just around this time a young boy was sent to him for instruction in the druidic arts. His name was Demna. He was an unusual boy, quick and intelligent, with a mass of gold-blonde hair, yet he spent his time telling the old man far-fetched stories. For example he claimed that he had lived the first five years of his life in a chamber cut in an oak tree, hiding there in secret with his grandmother and his puppy. Finn the Seer had seen this puppy, it was now a huge and fearsome hound called Bran who obeyed the young boy as if he were the King himself – so perhaps the story was true. But why the boy should have lived in such a way, and who he had been hiding from, remained a mystery.

The old man, however, warmed to the boy, enjoying his youth and energy. He was a quick learner so the old Seer taught him the *ogham* script, carving it out on stray branches cast by the mystical hazel trees. He also taught the boy to read prophetic signs in the patterns of clouds and the flight of birds. He encouraged him to summon powerful dreams in the old way, the two of them teasing out meanings together. He also told the boy the story of Aengus Og, the God of Love who lived in the Boyne Valley having tricked his old father, the Dagda, into giving it to him.

So much knowledge he imparted to him, yet all the while the Seer waited, guardian-like beside the pool with his rod poised, ready to catch the Salmon of Wisdom. And most days the two of them waited there together, the grey-haired old man and the young child with hair golden as the sun, attending on the pleasure of the hazel nuts and the mysterious Salmon.

Then one morning, when they arrived at the pool, they were astonished to see their prize waiting for them. One of the great Salmon was lying beached beside the Boyne, its crimson belly shimmering in the sunlight. The old Seer was overjoyed. He ordered Demna to take it away immediately and cook it, but cautioned him against eating any of it. But when Demna returned some time later with the cooked fish in his arms, the old Seer saw at once that a change had come over him.

'Demna,' he said angrily, 'did you eat any of the fish while you cooked it?'

'No', said the boy, 'but a blister rose on its skin and I pressed it down with my thumb, which scalded it, and then without thinking I put my thumb in my mouth to cool it.'

The old man sighed and was silent for a while.

'You told me you were called Demna,' he said at last, 'but have you any other name?'

Demna told him he had been nicknamed Finn, meaning the fair, because of his blonde hair. Then the old man realized with disappointment that this was the boy's destiny rather than his own and told Finn to eat the rest of the Salmon.

And after this, it is said, Finn only had to put his thumb under his tooth and immediately he was able to see the future and receive magical instruction. And, armed with these gifts, as a grown man he formed a great band called the *Fianna*, whose fame went round the whole of Ireland and whose high deeds of valour are remembered even to this day.

COMMENTARY

This story goes to the heart of Celtic spirituality. In it some of the Celts' most powerful symbols are combined with their deepest and most precious beliefs.

The story is set in the Boyne Valley, a highly potent place, home of the megalithic passage tombs, such as Newgrange. In this version the Salmon of Wisdom live in Fec's Pool, but in other accounts they live at the bottom of the Well of Inspiration, sometimes called

Connla's Well after the hero who was lured away to the Land of Youth by a fairy maiden. The Land of Youth lies under the sea, so it is possible that the Salmon of Wisdom were located beneath two kinds of water and a magical land, which suggests that they were believed to lie at the meeting point between the two worlds and even at the springs of creation itself.

The Salmon of Wisdom

In the story of 'Culhwch and Olwen' in the *Mabinogion*, the salmon is the most ancient creature consulted in the quest to find Mabon, and it is he who finds him. The salmon is, therefore, a symbol of ancient wisdom. It is unique, being able to survive both in fresh water and in the sea. It also shows great endurance, swimming long distances up rivers without sustenance to find its spawning grounds. Then, after spawning, it dies. The qualities of courage and self-sacrifice are demonstrated by its lifestyle. It also seemed hermit-like, having a habit of hiding in apparent contemplation, which made it difficult to catch. To the Celts the salmon was special among fish and they considered all fish to be spiritually symbolic. In this they were not alone. Ancient Egyptian and Greek mystery cults used bread and wine and fish in their rituals as emblems of the material, emotional and spiritual. Christianity also adopted the fish as a symbol of Christ, who chose fishermen for his disciples and even ate fish in his resurrected state. The Celts considered fish to be one of the treasures of the waters and gifts of the Great Mother.

The well and the hazel tree

Water is the very precondition of life. In Egyptian myth the Primeval Waters were believed to contain the seed of millions of beings. Both Mesopotamian and Celtic cultures believed there was a deep abyss of water under the surface of the world and it was this that issued in wells and springs and was the primal source of creation. It also represents the feminine and the unconscious. In fact the fish has sometimes been considered a phallic symbol in a feminine element, its prolific powers of reproduction giving it an added force of life and fertility. Taken together with the power of water, it becomes a symbol of regeneration.

The symbolism of the hazel is completely Celtic. All trees were sacred to the Celts and each had particular powers. The druids carried hazel rods because the hazel was considered the tree of inspiration and was sometimes called the poet's tree. It was also a tree of knowledge, but of knowledge that was divinely inspired. The hazel was also connected with immortality, so it is not surprising that its fruit should contain the most sacred and divinely inspired art, that of poetry. The Celts revered the word so much they would not write anything down but instead committed the equivalent of vast texts to memory.

Mystical numbers

Symbolically, numbers have always been very important. Three was a magical number for the Celts and its multiple, nine, was therefore the most potent number for them. The nine hazel trees signify a place of supreme importance. Also the number nine links with the nine months of pregnancy which is also seen as the engendering of the creative inner child. Number five, as in the number of salmon, is the number of essence and existence. In mythical terms it relates to the underlying structure of the psyche and of nature. It is the fifth element, achieved when the four main elements of the psyche are combined. It denotes wholeness and integration. The Salmon therefore symbolize the underlying truth that lies beneath changing appearances.

This myth contains all that is dearest to the Celts, the spiritual, the creative, the inspired, the place between this world and the Otherworld, the most sacred number, the oldest, wisest and most potent sea creature, the druid and the hero.

Individuation

In modern psychological terms, this story concerns the process of individuation. Jung has said that the individual must separate himself from the herd in order to distinguish his conscious ego from his unconscious. The purpose of this is for him to relate to his conscious ego, understand, own and respect his own individual personality and then, knowing himself, reconnect to society. This process involves seeking out his own treasure within his psyche, actualizing it and then relating back to the collective unconscious. The self is the inner treasure, the Salmon of Knowledge. The ego must seek it out, ingest its wisdom and put it to work in the world, for integration and individuation to occur. But in order to find the self, the ego must wait for wisdom to surface from the unconscious. When Finn eats the Salmon of Knowledge, he effectively marries the conscious with the unconscious, the spiritual with the physical. In this story the process of individuation is magically speeded up for him.

Youth and age

The relationship between the old man and the young boy is also important. As a druid, the old man is a particularly appropriate symbol of wisdom, knowledge and divination. His studying for many years has given him a learned wisdom, his practice of the high arts has given him prophetic powers, but he still seeks divine inspiration, that special knowledge that comes as a flash of lightning and is a gift from the gods.

In some ways, because of a lifetime of preparation, the old druid is ripe for such knowledge. Wisdom traditionally comes in the second half of life when riches and material wealth have already been acquired and the individual begins looking beyond such things. But the symbolism of the opposition of age with youth is very telling, for the young child is also poised at a very receptive time. He contains vital forces within him that are not yet realized but are seeking expression, and in his receptivity he is closer to the old man than he would be at a later point in his life. For whereas youth transforms into old age, old age itself transforms back into youth because it begins to produce the fruit of its work. Finn the Seer may have been disappointed that he was not to be the recipient of the divine knowledge himself, but, instead, he was the enabler, the necessary agent in the empowering of the child.

This story also celebrates the union of opposites: youth and age; conscious and unconscious; learning and intuition; masculine and feminine; temporal and spiritual. In order to become a hero, Finn needs a balance between intuition and worldly skills. He needs to know how to fight and he needs to be wise. It is rare to be able to combine the best of age and youth at any one time. Yet this is what the whole, rounded individual requires.

6 THE SORROWS OF DEIRDRE

This is the most well known of the Three Tragic Stories of Erin, the others being 'The Fate of the Children of Lir' and 'The Fate of the Children of Turenn'. There are several versions of this story, the earliest being found in the Book of Leinster. The tale belongs to the Ulster Cycle, also known as the Red Branch Cycle because it tells of the exploits of the hero Cuchulainn and his Red Branch warriors. It is included in the great saga known as the *Tain Bo Cuailnge*. Although Cuchulainn himself is not featured in this story, it serves to explain the defection of his great fellow warrior Fergus mac Roth to Queen Medb of Connacht.

Felim, son of Daill, was the chief storyteller of Conchobor, King of Ulster. One day he held a great feast, inviting Conchobor as his chief guest. The king attended with his retinue, which included the Druid Cathbad and the fearsome Fergus mac Roth along with other fierce warriors of the Red Branch. The bread and roasted meat went round and the wine flowed. Felim's wife, although heavily pregnant, was filling the drinking horns and generally waiting on the company. Then, as the evening turned to night, she took her leave and was crossing the courtyard on her way to the women's quarters when suddenly a great scream came from her womb which was so loud it echoed all round the hall. As one man, the warriors leaped up at the sound, standing face to face with their hands on their swords. Felim's wife ran to the Druid Cathbad and waited trembling while he placed his hand on her belly. The baby stormed and writhed like a wild thing beneath his hand. Then Cathbad spoke:

'It is a girl within your womb, a woman who cries out. She has curling golden hair and her eyes are slow and grey-pupilled. Her cheeks are as the foxgloves, purple in hue and the jewels of her teeth are bright as snow, her lips red as blood. She is destined to marry a king, but, because of her, three great heroes will die and there will be great slaughter in Ulster. This child shall be called Deirdre for she brings evil to the land.'

As he pronounced these words, Felim's wife fell down in great agony and the child was born. Then there was a great uproar and some of the warriors demanded that the child should be killed instantly. Indeed, many leaped up and would have killed it there and then if King Conchobor had not stopped them. He rose and shouted over the tumult, pledging that he himself would wed her when she was of age and thereby prevent this curse, and that meanwhile he would take care of her and hide her from the world. In the morning he departed taking the baby with him.

He built her a house on the edge of the palace grounds which had no windows to the back of it and a high wall cutting it off from the rest of the palace. There Deirdre was raised by foster-parents and the only companions she was allowed were her tutor and Levarcam the poetess.

The years passed and the only visitors the girl received were the King and Cathbad the Druid. But as winter followed autumn and summer followed spring, slowly she began to turn into a beautiful young woman. When she was 14 years old and just awakening to the possibilities of love, Conchobor made plans for the wedding.

One morning, seeing the blood of a butchered calf on the snow and a raven drinking it, Deirdre said, 'I could love a man who had hair as black as the raven's, cheeks as red as blood and a body as white as the snow.'

'Such a man lives in the king's court beyond the wall,' said Levarcam unguardedly. 'He is one of the three Sons of Usna. His name is Naoise and he is a head taller than his two brothers. They are all great warriors.'

Then Deirdre began to pine for sight of him until at last with great difficulty she contrived to encounter him in the forest as he walked alone without his brothers. She came in sight of him and made as if to pass him but he called out, 'Fair is the heifer that passes by me,' to which she replied, 'The young heifers will be eager in a place where there are no bulls.'

He moved towards her, not recognizing her but guessing who she must be. He came level with her and said quietly, 'But the bull of the whole province, the king himself is assigned to you.'

'I would choose a younger bull such as yourself,' she replied, looking him full in the eye.

He shook his head. 'You may not,' he said, 'because of Cathbad's prophecy.'

'Do you mean to refuse me then?' said Deirdre, seizing him by the ears. 'Because if so I will give you two ears of shame and ridicule unless you take me as your wife!'

Then Naoise let out a great cry and his brothers came running to him. When they heard of his plight they mourned that evil would come of the union, but they also agreed that he could not be disgraced in this way, so they vowed to accompany him and Deirdre in self-exile to Alba.

So Deirdre stole away with Naoise and his brothers, Aidan and Ainnli, and journeyed to Alba. There they lived as fugitives, hunted by Conchobor's men until at last the King of Alba offered them protection, glad to have such warriors in his country. Yet they were careful to hide Deirdre from his sight, because her great beauty was a danger to them.

Now the King of Alba was looking for a wife, and one day his steward caught sight of Deirdre as she sat in the hut and told the King of her breathtaking beauty. The King then sent the steward to woo her for him and contrived to send the three brothers on more and more dangerous exploits in the hope of killing them, but such was their prowess that they always survived. But when word came to Deirdre that the King was plotting to murder them, she persuaded them to escape to the highlands and islands where they fended for themselves, living off the land by hunting and fishing.

When news of their situation reached Ulster, King Conchobor finally offered to pardon them and invite them back to court. The other warriors of the Red Branch were overjoyed at this proposal. But the wily old king first asked Conall and Cuchulainn what they would do if anyone were to hurt the Sons of Usna while under their protection. Both answered that they would slay anyone who touched them. He then asked the same question of Fergus mac Roth, who replied that he would do the same except if it was the King himself. He swore that he could never injure the King. Pleased with this answer, Conchobor sent Fergus to Deirdre and the Sons of Usna charging him to bring them straight back and not let them eat or drink anything until they reached his court.

So, taking his two sons with him, Fergus set out for Alba. When they arrived at the lonely hut by the shore, he hailed loudly. Deirdre was immediately wary, sensing danger and tried to pretend there was no one outside, but Arden went out, and when he saw it was his kinsman Fergus he fell on his neck, kissing him like a brother. All the warriors embraced with tears of joy, but Deirdre was troubled. She told them that she had had a dream the previous night in which three birds came from Conchobor's palace at Emain Macha with three drops of honey in their beaks, but that they flew back with three drops of blood. 'I fear honey is the sweet message of the false man,' she said. But that night Fergus persuaded the three brothers that Conchobor was genuine in his forgiveness. In the morning Deirdre wept and sang a long lament over the beauty of Alba, of the highlands and islands that she was leaving, the vale of Eiti, the milking house of the sun, where she raised her first house in the wood, the vale of Laidh where she dined on fish and venison and the fat of the badger, and the Bay of Droighin where the waves lap over pure sand. 'I would never have come from it had I not come with my love,' she sang as the ship approached to take them to Erin.

As soon as they reached the shores of Erin, Conchobor sent a chieftain to invite them to dine at his house. This was the beginning of the treachery. Fergus was under *geis* to accept the hospitality of any chieftain through whose land he passed. At the same time the others were bound by an oath not to eat or drink or tarry anywhere until they reached the court of the king. So Fergus put them in the care of his two sons, but Deirdre was even more troubled and saw a further omen, a dark cloud like a blood-clot hanging in the sky above them. The three brothers, however, still refused to believe her and they journeyed on.

Finally, as they were nearing the court she said: 'If the king invites us directly to his palace all is well, but if he lodges us in the House of the Red Branch, he intends treachery against us.' Then Conchobor put off receiving them, sending them to the House of the Red Branch on the pretext that it was better stocked than his palace at Emain Macha. While they lodged there, he sent Levarcam to visit them, charging her to tell him if Deirdre was still as beautiful as ever. But Levarcam warned them of their danger and told them to barricade themselves in and wait for Fergus to return. Then she reported back to the king that because of her troubles and difficulties and rough life, Deirdre had entirely lost her looks. Then the king was pleased and felt his jealousy subsiding. But as he continued feasting and drank yet more wine he thought about Deirdre again and decided to send Trendorn, a chieftain whose family had been killed by Naoise, to report on her.

When he arrived, Trendorn found the house barred and bolted so he climbed up to look through a small window that was still unfastened, near the top of the wall. There he looked down on Naoise and Deirdre as they were playing chess. Deirdre felt the look and cried out. Naoise hurled a silver chessman at the opening with such force it took out Trendorn's eye. The chieftain ran back to the king, his eye gushing blood, declaring that the sight of Deirdre was the most beautiful thing in this world and that he would gladly have risked his other eye for the chance of gazing longer on her.

Then, his jealousy flaring up again, Conchobor summoned his troops to besiege the house. The Sons of Usna and the two sons of Fergus held out for as long as they could until one of Fergus' sons was slain and the other was bought off by the promise of large bribes of land from the king. Early the next morning the three brothers and Deirdre fled from the house and were well on their way when news of their escape was brought to Conchobor.

Then Conchobor asked Cathbad the Druid to help him. Cathbad agreed on condition that Conchobor gave his solemn oath that once he had Deirdre back he would not harm the Sons of Usna. The King gave his solemn pledge to this. So Cathbad caused a deep sea to appear with tumultuous waves so that the brothers had to abandon their weapons in order to swim through it. Then the sea miraculously disappeared and Conchobor's soldiers captured them unarmed and took them to Conchobor, who gave orders that the three of them be beheaded. None of his followers would perform the deed. Finally Eoghan, a former enemy who wished to make peace with the King, offered to do it, and cut off the heads of Naoise and his two brothers in one stroke.

Then Cathbad the Druid cursed Emain Macha and the whole province of Ulster because Conchobor had broken his solemn oath. He also cursed Conchobor's house, prophesying that none of his descendants would ever possess the great palace of Emain Macha.

In time, his curse was fulfilled. Fergus mac Roth joined the enemies of Ulster because of the treachery of the King and the curse on the province resulted in the great wars with Connacht. But while the curse still hung on Cathbad's lips and all these things were yet to come, Deirdre, distracted with grief, tore her hair and her clothes and kissed the wounds and drank the blood of her dead love. Then, calling on the 'three falcons of the Mount of Culan', the 'three lions of the wood of the cave' and the 'three dragons of the fort of Monadh', she uttered a long dirge for the death of the Sons of Usna. Then, pitching herself into their grave, she died on top of their bodies and was buried with them.

But some say that Deirdre lived on and was taken to the palace by King Conchobor but that for a whole year she neither raised her head from her knee, nor slept, nor ate nor smiled until, angered by her behaviour, the King asked her who she most hated in the world.

'You,' she replied. 'And after you, Eoghan, who killed Naoise and his brothers.'

'Then', said Conchobor, 'you shall go to Eoghan for a year and see what he makes of you.'

So Deirdre was put into a chariot and driven between the two men she most hated in the world and the look she gave them before fixing her stare on the ground was, said Conchobor, 'like the eye of a ewe between two rams'. Then Deirdre waited until they were driving past a large boulder, whereupon she threw herself out of the chariot and dashed her head against it, spilling her brains.

Romano-Celtic pipe-clay statuette of a triple-aspected goddess

COMMENTARY

This is perhaps the most poignant and well known of all Celtic stories. Originally part of a long heroic saga, the *Tain Bo Cuailnge*, the tale was able to stand alone because of the powerful figure of Deirdre. It was passed down orally and entered the Scottish Gaelic folk tradition where Deirdre was made the child of Malcolm Harper and his wife.

Deirdre as goddess figure

The character of Deirdre overpowers all others in the story. She evidently has Otherworldly attributes. She shrieks prophetically inside her mother's womb, she is depicted before birth as beautiful and wild, and she has the power to lay a *geis* or injunction on

Naoise. Further demonstrations of her divine nature include her ability to have prophetic dreams and to see portents in the sky. She seems, therefore, to be a goddess figure and a close examination of this triangular love story suggests that it reflects the ancient theme of the death and rebirth of the solar hero and the refertilization of the earth.

In this interpretation Deirdre represents the goddess figure of ancient matriarchal fertility myths, symbol of springtime, youth and the regeneration of the earth. The old King, who symbolizes winter or the death of the old year, is challenged by the virile young warrior who seeks to take her from him and thus refertilize the earth. In Deirdre's case, the tragedy lies in the fact that the natural order is broken because the goddess's new young consort is killed by the old one and so the earth cannot be renewed and replenished.

This theme is a familiar one, especially where triangular love stories are concerned. It can be seen in the story of 'Lleu and Blodeuwedd' in the Third Branch of the *Mabinogion* and also in the love story of 'Diarmuid and Grainne', where it develops into a conflict between love and honour, prefiguring the love conflicts of the Arthurian Romances. But Deirdre differs from these other nature goddess figures because she invites our pity.

Deirdre of the Sorrows

Deirdre is the embodiment of grief. She has been called 'Deirdre of the Sorrows' because in her lamentation over the bodies of the three heroes, she evokes the eternal image of the suffering woman, both as wife and mother. She also represents the anguish of the soul. In this respect Deirdre mourning over the Sons of Usna prefigures the powerful image of the *pietà*, the Virgin Mary lamenting over the body of Christ.

Although Deirdre is apparently barren in the story, her identification with the Virgin Mary as *Mater Dolorosa* strongly suggests a mother figure. More ancient goddess figures who prefigured Mary, such as Isis and Cybele, show a confusion of consort and son. Isis resurrects her husband Osiris, who becomes interchangeable with her son Horus; and Cybele becomes her own son's lover. Rather than being incestuous, on a symbolic level this demonstrates the permanence of the Great Mother and the turning cycle of the male as newborn child and dying consort. In her lamenting at the graveside of the three brothers, Deirdre foreshadows Grainne simultaneously mourning her dead husband and three dead babies.

Whereas the earlier nature goddesses were detached, Deirdre reveals the compassionate side of the female who is emotionally involved in the sacrificial principle of death within life. But Deirdre's mourning is particularly poignant and human because she did not initiate the death of her consort. Deirdre's tragedy lies in the fact that she has been denied her powers of regeneration and fallen victim to those who believe they should control her. She therefore mourns not only the death of Naoise but also the death of her own life-giving power. This is why she kills herself.

The bull in the *Tain Bo Cuailnge*

Some scholars think the tale of Deirdre was only interpolated into the *Tain* to explain the defection of Fergus mac Roth from King Conchobor of Ulster to Queen Medb of Connacht. But perhaps the position of this tale here has a deeper purpose. The theme of the *Tain* concerns the war waged over a magical bull. The bull was a powerful symbol of regeneration, prominent both in Greek and Celtic myth. Its crescent-shaped horns represented the goddess who sat astride its masculine powers of strength and fertility. The magical bull of the *Tain* can be seen as representing the regenerative principle which has been stolen from the goddess by the new patriarchy. She fights to reclaim it, knowing that if her link with it is severed, the earth will cease to be renewed. The personification of Deirdre as an image of the defeated goddess thus becomes a fitting prelude to the saga.

Positive anima

At a psychological level, like the Virgin Mary, Deirdre is a manifestation of the ennobled positive anima, or inner feminine figure. This figure forms the link between man's rational side and his true inner values. When he persists in ignoring her, as Creon does with Antigone in Greek myth, he risks losing what is most dear to him. But the figure of Deirdre, like that of the Virgin Mary, is disempowered, being the split-off fair aspect of the anima. Through fear and ignorance she has been divorced from her dark side and thus from her links with the earth and fecundity.

Triplicity

The Celts represented the goddess as triple-aspected, having three faces, those of maiden, mother and crone, to symbolize the three phases of life. In the tale of Deirdre, the three Sons of Usna are depicted as a heroic equivalent of the triple-aspected goddess. They move as one and are killed together, the two lesser brothers having no individual personalities. They are therefore aspects of Naoise, serving to reinforce his prowess. The name of Naoise survives, however, in Loch Ness. Alba is the old name for Scotland.

7 DIARMUID AND GRAINNE

This Irish and Scottish tale is part of the Fenian Cycle. The earliest mention of it is in a listing in the Book of Leinster, where Grainne is called Ailbe. According to Douglas Hyde there is a copy of the full story written around 1660 in the Reeves Collection in the Royal Irish Academy. A later version is found, edited and translated, in the third volume of the Ossianic Society by Standish O'Grady and another by Joyce in *Old Celtic Romances*.

Early one morning the great chieftain and warrior Finn mac Cumhail was walking on the grassy plain outside his palace. Oisin, his son, and Dering, his druid, saw him and went out to ask him what was the matter. Finn said that ever since his wife had died he had been unable to sleep from loneliness.

'Oh, but that's easily remedied!' the two men cried, 'Find another woman to marry! Choose whoever you like from the whole of Ireland and we will get her for you.' 'In fact', said Dering, 'I know the very woman for you. Grainne, the daughter of King Cormac mac Art!'

'But', said Finn, 'there are bad relations between myself and her father. I would rather not ask him for her myself.'

'Then we will go for you,' said the two men and immediately set off for Tara.

When they arrived, they put Finn's offer to Cormac, who told them that so far his daughter had refused all suitors. He went to her chamber, however, to ask her.

'Grainne,' he said, 'would you consider marrying Finn mac Cumhail?'

To his surprise she replied, 'Why not, if you think him fit enough for a son-in-law?'

So it was arranged that at the end of two weeks Finn would come for Grainne.

After that a great wedding feast was prepared and Finn arrived, bringing with him the most daring warriors from his famous warband, the *Fianna*. When the feast was underway, having already appraised Grainne's beauty, Finn decided to test her famous wit and began a riddling game with her.

'What is hotter than fire?' he asked.

Quick as a flash she replied, 'That would be a woman's choosing between two men.'

'What runs swifter than the wind?'

'A woman's thinking between two men.'

'What is sharper than a sword?'

'The hatred of an enemy.'

'What is softer than swans' down?'

'The touch of a palm on a cheek.'

'What is whiter than the purest snow?'

'The truth.'

'What is blacker than the raven?'

'Death.'

This interchange satisfied Finn, but Grainne was troubled, aware that she had spoken of more than she knew.

Later that evening Dara, the poet, who was sitting close to Grainne was surprised when she suddenly asked him,

'Why are Finn and the Fianna here?'

'If you do not know that, it is hardly for me to tell you,' he replied. 'He has come to take you as his wife.'

'But he is older than my father,' she said. 'It would be better if I were given to his son Oisin or even his grandson, Oscar.'

Then, looking round at the company, she asked Dara to tell her the names of the other warriors. He pointed out several of the most noble and then she asked:

'Who is that man with the reddened cheeks and the dark curl on his forehead?'

'That', said Dara, 'is Diarmuid, the fairest of the heroes and the mark beneath his curl is his love-spot.'

Then he told her that Diarmuid had once been hunting late in the woods with three of the Fianna. They had received shelter for the night in a rough-looking hut inhabited by an old man and his daughter. When a sheep climbed onto the table, they were unable to wrestle it off, yet it was led away easily by a black cat. They were told that the sheep represented the world and the cat represented death, the only power that could overcome it. Finally, when they tried to entice the beautiful young girl to bed, she told them that they could no longer possess her because her name was Youth. However, she gave Diarmuid a magical mark which, she said, would ever after draw upon him the love of women.

After hearing this, Grainne understood that she had fallen under Diarmuid's spell and would never escape. She told her servants to bring her the great golden drinking cup. She put a sleeping draught into it so that, as it went round, the warriors fell asleep one by one, until only Oisin and Diarmuid were left awake. Softly, she stole across to Oisin and asked if he would take her for his wife, but he refused in loyalty to Finn. Then she asked Diarmuid and he too refused. At this, Grainne drew herself up to her full height and her eyes blazed into his like molten stars.

'Then I will put a *geis* on you,' she said. 'Come away with me tonight so that I may escape marrying Finn.'

'That is an evil thing you do,' said Diarmuid, 'and no good will come of it. I beg you to think again.'

'I will not!' said Grainne.

'Then it is a heavy burden you have put on me,' sighed Diarmuid. 'In any case, since Finn holds the keys to the palace tonight, we are not able to escape.'

'Then we can go out from my wicket gate.'

'But', said Diarmuid, 'I am under *geis* never to go through a wicket gate.'

Grainne was scornful. 'Everyone knows that you have a special ability to vault over any obstacle. Take your spear and vault over the castle walls.'

Then Diarmuid desperately sought the advice of his fellow warriors. While pitying his plight they all agreed that he must not break the *geis* that had been laid on him. So Diarmuid armed himself and leapt over the palace wall, and he and Grainne began their flight together.

When Finn awoke next morning and found his bride gone, he stormed and raged and set off in hot pursuit. It was fearful to be hunted by Finn because he had a great magical ability. When he placed his thumb in his mouth he was able to see whatever he wished, however far away it might be. But Diarmuid had thought of a way of fooling him. When they stopped to sleep on the shore he put leaves beneath their heads so Finn would think they were in a forest, and when they stopped in a forest he placed sand beneath them so Finn would think they were on the seashore. In this way they held off his pursuit successfully for many days. But even so, Finn would always come upon their hideout. So Diarmuid left behind him signs, a whole fish or a piece of unbroken bread, as a token to Finn that Grainne was still untouched. But Grainne was insulted by this display of false loyalty. One day when she was splashed while crossing a river, she exclaimed that the water was bolder than Diarmuid, having touched her more intimately.

'And you call yourself a hero of the Fianna!' she added scornfully.

This taunt was too much for Diarmuid, who laid her down on the river bank and took her there and then for his wife.

The couple fled for many months hotly pursued by Finn and his men. But because of his extraordinary prowess Diarmuid was always able to outwit or overcome his attackers. But, one day, they decided to take refuge in the forest of Dooros. This was where the Quicken Tree grew. It was an Otherworldly tree grown from a berry dropped by the *dé Dananns*, the fairy people who had once ruled Ireland. The berries tasted of honey and made anyone who ate them immediately joyful, and sometimes, it was said, they could restore youth.

But the Quicken Tree was guarded by Sharvan the Surly, a giant of the old race who had a flaming red eye in the middle of his forehead and a club bound to him by an iron chain. He was feared throughout the land and no warrior dared come into his forest. Undaunted, however, Diarmuid went in and found the giant at the foot of the tree and asked his permission to live in the forest with Grainne. This was grudgingly granted but only on condition that they left the quicken berries untouched. So Diarmuid built a hut and he and Grainne lived there in safety for some time until Grainne became pregnant and was overcome by a great desire to taste the quicken berries.

Meanwhile Finn sent two chiefs of Leinster into the forest, instructing them either to kill Diarmuid or bring back a fistful of quicken berries. Diarmuid overcame them easily and bound them. Then he asked the giant for some quicken berries for Grainne. The giant refused and aimed his club at Diarmuid, but Diarmuid sprang out of the way, snatched up the club and killed the giant with three great blows. Then he gave some berries to Grainne and a handful to the chiefs to take back to Finn.

When the chiefs returned, Finn took one sniff of the berries and said he could smell the hand of Diarmuid on them. Then, hearing the giant was dead, he set out again in pursuit of the couple. Diarmuid waited for him in the Quicken Tree, hiding with Grainne in its topmost branches. When Finn arrived at the tree, he sat down under it and called for a chessboard so he and his son Oisin could play a game. When Oisin was in danger of losing, Diarmuid, observing from the treetop, adroitly sent a berry down so that it hit the piece that should be moved. Three times he did this so that Oisin won three games against Finn. At last Finn said that it was hardly surprising that Oisin had won considering that he had Diarmuid to advise him. Then Diarmuid spoke up and announced himself, after which he pulled Grainne towards him and gave her three kisses. Finn responded by offering great honours to any of his men who would climb the tree and bring Diarmuid down. All refused except for Garva, whose father had been killed by Diarmuid's father, and who wished to take revenge.

As Garva began to climb the tree, Aengus Og, the god of love, became aware of the lovers' predicament and went straight to them. He had a special relationship with Diarmuid, having been his foster-father, so he offered to carry them both away with him.

Diarmuid, however, wanted to fight his own way out, so Aengus took Grainne and carried her to safety at his palace on the River Boyne. Meanwhile Diarmuid fought off Garva and his relatives and Oscar begged Finn to make peace with him. While they argued, Diarmuid made a great leap from the tree, landing beyond the ring of warriors. Then he began running and was joined by Oscar and, because the Fianna were reluctant to follow, they easily made their escape. After this Finn gave up pursuing the lovers and returned to his palace.

Sixteen years passed in which Diarmuid and Grainne lived in peace and raised four sons and a daughter. Then Grainne began to pine for sight of her father so she said to Diarmuid that it was a shame they had never been able to offer hospitality to either her father or Finn. Diarmuid was amazed to hear this, but Grainne insisted that all enmity had long been forgotten and that it was high time to invite everyone to a great feast. So messengers were sent with invitations and both Cormac and Finn accepted. They came with their men and feasted for a whole year with Diarmuid and Grainne.

Then, one morning, Diarmuid woke early to hear the sound of a hound yelping. Three times he heard it and then he determined to go out hunting. Grainne felt troubled and told him to take two magical weapons with him, the sword of Mannanan mac Lir and the spear of Aengus. But Diarmuid was scornful and instead took his own spear and sword.

He came to the mountain of Ben Bulben, where he met Finn, who said that, against his advice, his men had been hunting the famous Wild Boar of Ben Bulben, which even now might be bearing down on them. Finn suggested leaving the mountain but Diarmuid refused. Then Finn told him that he must because he was under *geis* never to hunt a boar. Diarmuid replied that he knew nothing of such a *geis*. So Finn told him that when he was fostered at Aengus' palace on the Boyne, an illegitimate child of his mother's was fostered alongside him. This so angered his father, Don, that, one day, when he was playing with the two boys and the other child ran between his legs, he squeezed him between his knees, crushing him to death. At this the steward of the house, who was the child's father, snatched up a druid's wand and with it turned the dead child into a wild boar, commanding it to take the life of Diarmuid in revenge.

'After which', said Finn, 'Aengus laid a *geis* on you never to hunt wild boar.'

But Diarmuid protested that he knew nothing of such a prohibition and would not turn back now for fear of the boar or any other wild beast. Then Finn left him alone on Ben Bulben. At once the boar came rushing towards him and Diarmuid tried both spear and sword against it but to no avail. The boar gashed his side deeply with its tusk, but at the same time Diarmuid drove the hilt of his sword through its brain. Then the Fianna came up and Finn with them and they found Diarmuid on the point of death. Finn gloated over Diarmuid and said it gave him pleasure to see his beautiful body so marred. But Diarmuid begged Finn to remember his glorious deeds in the *Fianna* and to bring him water from a nearby well and heal him, for he knew Finn had this ability.

Then Finn went and drew water in his hands and came up to Diarmuid, but let the water run through his fingers onto the grass rather than heal him. Again the dying man pleaded with him and again Finn brought the water but again let it fall to the ground. Then Diarmuid prevailed on him a third time and Finn went and brought the water and sprinkled it on Diarmuid's body, healing it perfectly, but too late, for he was already dead.

Then Oscar upbraided Finn and told him it was a terrible thing for him to have let such a hero as Diarmuid die and he himself remain alive. Then Oscar, Oisin, Finn and Caoilte threw their mantles over Diarmuid and retreated with the rest of the *Fianna*, for Finn feared the coming of Aengus Og and the Tuatha dé Danann. They made their way to Grainne's palace, Finn leading Diarmuid's faithful staghound, Mac an Cuill.

Grainne was looking over the ramparts anxiously waiting for the return of her husband. When she saw Finn with Diarmuid's staghound, she began to fear the worst. She leaned out, desperately hoping to see Diarmuid and, being heavily pregnant, she toppled over and fell to the ground. In the shock of the fall she gave birth to three dead sons.

Oisin then commanded his father and the *Fianna* to leave. As they were going, Grainne asked for Diarmuid's hound and when Finn refused, Oisin took it from him and gave it to her.

When Grainne finally realized that Diarmuid was indeed dead, she let out a great and piteous cry which penetrated the whole palace. At that the whole household assembled. When they understood that their lord was dead they let out three great shouts of grief which ascended as far as the Heavens and in the wastes beneath the Earth.

Then Grainne commanded her people to go to Ben Bulben and bring back her husband's body.

And there the story ends, but there are some who say that Aengus insisted on taking Diarmuid back with him to Brug na Boyne where he breathed a soul into him so that Diarmuid might talk with him a little each day.

COMMENTARY

In this story Finn comes across as a jealous and formidable tyrant. Yet he had eaten the Salmon of Wisdom (see page 35) and was a renowned hero with a poetic and druidic understanding. Although these attributes are still apparent they are overridden by a kind of hubris. Like Shakespeare's King Lear, Finn imagines he can control those around him when, really, the time has come to give way to the new order of things. He also uses his magical gifts in a wrong cause. These gifts are akin to divine attributes and show that Finn himself may also be a euhemerized deity. Whereas in the Welsh story 'Math, Son of Mathonwy', Math has a supernatural gift of hearing, Finn has an equivalent gift of seeing. This is linked to his thumb because it was this that he burned when he cooked the Salmon of Wisdom. A further tale says that he caught his thumb in the door of a fairy *sidhe*, when he was escaping from it. He received his gift of healing when carrying water in his hands, at the same time as the other, and both gifts came from the Boyne.

Grainne

As the daughter of the High King of Tara, and therefore of all Ireland, Grainne is a powerful representation of the Goddess of Sovereignty (see page 74). Her riddling contest with Finn suggests that she has experienced druidic initiation, for this was a characteristic way in which druids spoke with each other. That she possessed special intuitive knowledge is also suggested by a story in which Cormac is tricked by Mananan mac Lir, the sea god, into exchanging his wife and children for a magical apple branch. They are taken to the Otherworld, where Cormac eventually finds them. On his way he passes the Fountain of Inspiration and it is possible that, during her time in the Otherworld, Grainne has drunk from it.

Her contest with Finn is the turning point in the story. Prior to this she has unthinkingly accepted her fate, seeming to be in a dreamlike, passive state when her father suggests her marriage to Finn. Because he and Finn had been at enmity with each other, presumably she had never seen him and may not have been aware of his age. Also Cormac might have urged the betrothal in order to end the enmity. In any case, from Grainne's point of view, as the most famous hero in the land, Finn must have seemed a good choice. But in the riddling game Grainne finds her own mind. She discovers she loves another man and, in choosing him, must follow her own truth and risk the consequences. Like Deirdre, she submits to the power of love.

Love

Although this story in many ways echoes that of 'Deirdre and the Sons of Usna', there are important differences. While the power of love seems to be the central theme of both stories, in 'Diarmuid and Grainne' love is fostered supernaturally. Having been brought up by Aengus Og, the God of Love, and marked with the love-spot, Diarmuid becomes the protagonist in this story. Grainne is first spellbound by Diarmuid before she puts him under *geis*.

Aengus Og is very prominent in this story. He is apparently 'more beautiful than beauty'. He is the son of the Dagda, the Great God of the Tuatha dé Danann (the fairy people). Intriguingly, Aengus was born outside time. This was because the Dagda had an illicit relationship with the Goddess Boann. In order to conceal her infidelity from her husband, the Dagda caused the sun to stand still for nine months until she had given birth to Aengus, whom she called the Bright Child. Aengus, after discovering who his father was, managed to persuade the Dagda to bestow on him the palace of the Boyne. This is the great monument of Newgrange with an upper chamber and passage for the sun to strike through at the winter solstice (see page 20). Aengus is therefore associated with the sun as well as with love and eternal youth. Like Apollo, and also like the Dagda, he played a magic harp whose music was irresistible. According to Lady Gregory he was also known as 'the Disturber', because cattle were frightened by him and ran away when he approached.

The power of love as a disturber is a strong element in the story. It awakens Grainne to her true nature and sexuality and it forces Diarmuid into a terrible conflict between his duty to Finn and his obedience to Grainne's demands. For a time he tries to please both, until Grainne at last secures his sexual favours.

Diarmuid

Diarmuid is a complex character. He is an exemplary member of the *Fianna*, possessing some of the finest battle skills in the band. He is also very beautiful and already has quite a reputation with women, which is explained or excused by his love-spot. It is reported that before being fostered by Aengus Og, he was brought up by Manannan mac Lir in the Otherworld or Land of Promise (see pages 91–3). He is therefore something of a fairy child and would seem to have been trained not just for war but for love. His role in the love triangle is similar to that of Lancelot in the Arthurian cycle, who was also brought up on an Otherworldly island, by the Lady of the Lake.

Diarmuid is also a much more fully realized character than Naoise. In this respect he and Grainne are equally strong. Diarmuid is the protagonist but he presents difficulties on the flight by refusing to sleep with Grainne. But in this he is also resisting his own development. By refusing to leave by the wicket gate and leaping over the wall, he leaps symbolically over a boundary and begins a new stage of life. Joseph Campbell has noticed that the flight was a common motif of hero stories, together with the trick of throwing or leaving diversionary objects behind in order to slow down the hunter. By leaving untouched loaves and fishes behind him in a strangely Christian testimony to her purity, Diarmuid is curiously reversing this technique and inviting Finn to retrieve his unravished bride. However, once he has slept with Grainne, he changes and becomes bold enough to taunt Finn by kissing her in front of him.

The Quicken Tree and the theme of youth

The story of Diarmuid and Grainne is much more sexually overt than that of Deirdre and Naoise but the greatest contrast between the women is that Grainne becomes pregnant while Deirdre does not. Grainne's pregnancy occurs during the lover's sojourn in the Forest of Dooros. This curious episode is reminiscent of the Garden of Eden with the forbidden fruit on the Tree of Life. As its name tells us, the Quicken Tree is a tree of life and 'quicken' also refers to pregnancy. The magical tree has been seeded by a berry from the Otherworld. Its fruit can bestow youth and thus immortality on those who eat it. The giant Sharvan is a guardian figure, but his chain and club demonstrate a Saturnian restrictiveness. He is therefore a symbol of the life-denying ego, that fights healthy change. He resembles other figures such as Atlas, who jealously guards his apples, or Ysbaddaden in the *Mabinogion*, who jealously guards his daughter. Sharvan here also relates to Finn, who will not relinquish his hold on youth and love and release the next generation.

The game of chess that Finn plays under the tree symbolizes the battle he is fighting with Diarmuid, who takes part in it by helping Oisin. Diarmuid wins it by dropping a quicken berry, which shows that he has the upper hand.

The theme of youth runs right through this story. Apart from the pervasive presence of Aengus, the ever-youthful god, there is the extraordinary tale of how Diarmuid got the love-spot. The symbolism in this tale is spelled out and the heroes are made to see that, for all their prowess, they can have no power to overthrow the world, escape death or hold onto youth. But, at the end, Diarmuid is supernaturally marked with the power of love by the Maiden of Youth, who is the female counterpart of Aengus Og.

The combination of youth and love undergirds the hero's destiny, so it is not surprising that he has several children and that he dies while still young enough to father more. The theme of fertility combined with that of love is, again, a very strong one in this story and differentiates Grainne from the figure of Deirdre. For it is Deirdre's barrenness that makes her story particularly poignant. An echo of her desolate state when she weeps over the grave of the three brothers is found when, in response to Diarmuid's death, Grainne gives birth to three dead sons.

Regeneration

Interestingly, unlike Lleu, and in spite of all his supernatural endowments, Diarmuid dies and is not resurrected. The only hint of any kind of resurrection is in the strange story of Aengus Og putting a soul into him on a daily basis so that he can talk to him. Aengus' palace of Brug na Boyne, being the seat of love, has been equated with the castle of the soul. In psychological terms the soul is linked to the anima, which in its positive form is an image of love. Love therefore has some powers in terms of the regeneration of the soul. But in this story, as with the head of Bran in the *Mabinogion*, there is only a token resurrection.

Even so, it is not as desolate as the ending of Deirdre and perhaps this is why a more prosaic ending was later added to it. In this, Grainne, after summoning her sons and bidding them undergo an arduous training in order to wreak revenge on Finn, is then won round by Finn who woos her with soft words until she consents to marry him. As she returns to his palace with him, she is greeted with a howl of derision from the Fianna. She then persuades her children to give up their vengeance on condition that they are given their father's place in the Fianna. After this she remains with Finn for the rest of his life.

Of course, this ending could also be a later Christianization of the story, in which the old Celtic vengeance gives way to Christian forgiveness, as in 'The Voyage of Maeldun'. But Grainne's more assertive character makes her change of heart believable. Although both Deirdre and Grainne are very powerful women who get their way by their goddess-like power of *geis*, it is Deirdre who remains in the mind as the great symbol of sorrow, while Grainne strikes a more modern note. She is the woman who uses her power to survive, who rides with love when it comes to her and yet is not above yielding to opportunity when it arises.

8 MATH, SON OF MATHONWY, PART I: THE BIRTH OF LLEU

This is the Fourth Branch or tale from the collection of ancient Welsh myths known as the *Mabinogion*, from the word *mab* meaning 'child'.

A great king called Math once ruled over the land of Gwynedd. He was a fair and wise man and was respected by his people. He was also something of a magician, but, besides his magical powers, he had one great attribute. He was able to hear the words of anyone in his kingdom, down to the merest whisper, if it were carried to him on the wind. But he was also subject to a strange prohibition: except when he was at war, he was unable to live unless his feet were cradled in the lap of a virgin.

Because of this prohibition Math was not able to make ordinary circuits of his land so instead he sent his nephews: Gwydion, the young magician, and his brother, Gilvaethwy. One day as they were travelling round Math's cantrevs Gwydion noticed that his brother had hardly eaten and was looking very pale. Gwydion asked him what the matter was. But Gilvaethwy refused to answer, only making signs of silence, shaking his head and putting his finger on his lips. When Gwydion pressed him, he mouthed:

'You know that I cannot speak without Math being able to hear me.'

Then Gwydion replied, 'Don't even try to utter your problem for I have guessed it.' Then he said softly: 'You desire Goewin, Math's virgin, don't you?'

Gilvaethwy sighed, thinking of the beautiful, untouched maiden who cradled the King's feet. With silent signals Gwydion promised to find a way to procure her for his brother. After that not another word was spoken between them concerning the matter.

On their return, Gwydion asked for an audience with Math and told him that he had heard of some remarkable animals that had just arrived in Dyfed, the land south of Gwynedd.

'What are they and where have they come from?' asked Math.

'They are called pigs and they come from Arawn, King of the Underworld. They are quite small and their flesh is more tender than that of oxen,' said Gwydion.

'Who owns them?' asked Math.

'Pryderi, King of Dyfed and Glamorgan,' said Gwydion. 'But give me leave to take a band of twelve men with me and we will go to Pryderi's court disguised as bards and ask for the animals.'

'What if he refuses you?' said Math.

'He won't,' said Gwydion, 'for I have a good plan.'

So Math sent Gwydion with his blessing.

When Gwydion arrived at Pryderi's court with Gilvaethwy and the ten other bards, the King welcomed them and invited them to dine with him. When they were seated, he asked for a story, and Gwydion, who was an expert storyteller, regaled the court with several tales which were very well received.

'Now,' said Gwydion, 'may I put in words to you a request that I have?'

Pryderi consented, so Gwydion said, 'Lord, I would ask you for the new animals which you have received from Arawn.'

The king replied, 'It is not in my power to give them to you, because I have made a pledge to my people that I will keep them until they have bred twice their number.'

'Perhaps I can make you rethink your pledge', said Gwydion, 'when I show you tomorrow what I can offer in exchange for them.'

That night Gwydion summoned up his magical arts. Before dawn broke he had conjured twelve stallions, decking them out with well-crafted golden saddles and bridles, together with twelve black greyhounds with white breasts, which he adorned with gold collars and leashes. Lastly, just as the first light of day appeared, he turned a handful of toadstools into twelve blazing gilded shields.

All these he presented to Pryderi and his court while the fairy gold upon them flashed and sparkled temptingly in the bright sunlight. Pryderi held a council to decide whether to exchange the pigs for these great gifts. In the end he decided to make the exchange, so Gwydion and his men departed with the precious pigs, Gwydion telling his men: 'Hurry, because the magic will only last a day!' So they journeyed swiftly back to Math.

When they returned, they found Math's people preparing for war. Pryderi had discovered the trick and was mustering his troops to do battle with Math and recover his pigs. So Math went out to meet him, accompanied by his two nephews. But after they camped the first night, the two brothers stole back to Math's castle, Caer Dathal. They found Goewin and her attendant women in Math's chamber and forced the women out at spearpoint. Then Gilvaethwy ravished the girl. Her screams were heard all over the castle, but no one could rescue her, for all the men were away at war.

The next day the two brothers returned to the army and joined battle with Pryderi. There was great slaughter on both sides but eventually Pryderi was forced to retreat and was pursued by Math's soldiers until they agreed to a truce. Fighting broke out again, however, so Pryderi offered to meet Gwydion in single combat. Math agreed to this, so the beguiled king and the young upstart magician fought each other long and hard until at last, with the aid of magic as well as skill, Gwydion killed Pryderi.

While Math and his army marched back to Caer Dathal, his two nephews quickly went off on their accustomed circuit of the cantrevs. On his return, Math called for his chamber to be prepared so that he might rest his feet in Goewin's lap. But she came to him dishevelled, her face pale and drawn, and said:

'Lord, you must find another virgin to hold your feet, for I am now a woman.'

Then she broke down and told him how she had been raped and dishonoured by his nephews while he was away. At this a great wrath rose up in Math. First, he pledged the distraught girl that he would compensate her by taking her as his wife, then he sent a command to his people throughout the kingdom not to supply his nephews with food or drink. The two men delayed returning to court for as long as possible, but in the end they were forced to come back through hunger and were immediately brought before Math.

'Good day to you, Lord,' they said.

'Well!' said Math 'And have you come to give me recompense?'

'Lord,' they replied, 'we are subject to your will.'

Math snorted. 'If it had been my will, I would not have lost so many warriors and weapons as I have done. You can never compensate me for my shame or for the death of Pryderi.'

He paused, and his great brows lifted while he shot a look like a spear's thrust at the two men.

'Since you have come to do my will,' he said, 'I shall begin my punishment of you.'

At this he took up his wand and struck Gilvaethwy with it, turning him into a hind. Then, as Gwydion was trying to escape, he caught hold of him and struck him too, so that he turned into a stag.

'There', he said. 'Since you have schemed together, now go and mate together and return to me in twelve months.'

A year later there was wild barking from the dogs outside the wall of Math's chamber. He sent to find out what the din was about and was told that three wild animals had come to court, a stag, a hind and a young fawn. Math went out to meet them and raised his wand.

'For the next twelve months', he said, 'you shall become wild hogs: the one that was a hind shall become a sow and the one that was a hind shall become a hog. Now go!'

But he transformed the fawn into a boy, had him baptized, and sent him to be fostered.

A further year went by and again there was a great barking from the palace dogs and the two wild swine returned with a young piglet. Again Math struck them with his wand, changed their sexes and, this time, turned them into wolves. But he transformed the piglet into an auburn-haired boy and sent him also to be fostered.

A further year passed and then the wolves returned with a wolf-cub. This time he changed all three into human form.

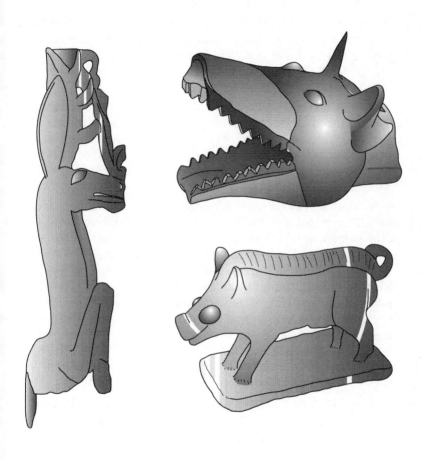

Celtic animal group (clockwise from left): stag found as offering in well (Germany); trumpet mouth in the form of a wolf's head (Spain); bronze pig figurine (England)

'You men have suffered much disgrace and punishment for the wrong you did me,' he said.

Then he commanded that they should be bathed and anointed. After that he welcomed them saying: 'You have made your peace and you shall regain my friendship.'

He invited them to dine with him and when they were seated he said: 'And now I shall ask your advice. Which virgin shall I take as my footholder?' Quick as a flash the wily Gwydion replied, 'My sister Arianrhod.'

Now Arianrhod was a proud and beautiful woman. She ruled over Caer Sidi, a magical palace that stood on an island and that contained the fiery seat of poetic inspiration. When she sat on a dais in her inner chamber, she was protected by three flowing fountains and by three rings of fire. She was a fiercely independent woman who claimed that her power rested in her virginity.

So Math sent Gwydion to his sister Arianrhod to see if she would be willing to become his footholder. The two siblings were very close, but it was a long time since they had seen each other. Arianrhod welcomed Gwydion with open arms and they strolled together in the palace grounds and made sport with one another. Then Gwydion brought her back with him to the court and presented her to Math. Arianrhod walked the length of the hall with her train of maidens behind her and stood haughtily before the king. Tall and queenly, she was dressed in robes so finely woven that they moved and glittered like the moon on water. The King was immediately aware of her worth, but before he could accept her as his footholder, he was obliged to ask her one thing.

'Lady,' he said, 'do I have your word that you are indeed a virgin?'

Arianrhod drew herself up and looked directly into Maths eyes. 'I am, my lord,' she said, 'as far as I am aware.'

Then Math took up his wand and laid it on the ground.

'Step over that,' he said, 'and I will know for sure.'

Arianrhod gathered up her fine skirts and lifted her foot to step over the wand. At once she let out a scream of pain as a yellow-haired baby boy fell from her womb. A hush of shock and horror fell on the court broken only by the crying of the child. As soon as she was sufficiently recovered, Arianrhod turned and ran from the hall and, as she did so, a further small form fell from her, but what it was no one could say, for, quicker than sight, Gwydion snatched it up, swathed it in a velvet scarf and carried it away. Then, coming to himself, Math took charge, naming the baby Dylan and sending him to be baptized. But when the child was taken to the sea, he turned into a sea creature and wriggled away – as well he might, for his name means 'Son of the Wave'.

Arianrhod, meanwhile, fled back to her castle, while Gwydion kept to himself. He had placed the swaddled object in an oak chest at the foot of his bed which he had prepared with spells and which he kept closed for a number of months. One morning as he lay awake he heard a small cry from inside the chest. He opened it and discovered a baby boy pushing aside the velvet scarf and flailing his arms, waiting to be picked up. He took up the boy, rocking and soothing him. Then he put him with a wetnurse who looked after him for a year.

At the end of the year, it seemed as if the child had grown out of all proportion. He had dark hair and green eyes which held wisdom beyond his age. By the end of the second year, the child was big enough to attend court. There he was received with great fondness by Gwydion, who treated him as if he were his own child and when the lad was only four years old, he had the stature and maturity of a child of eight.

It was about this time that Gwydion judged it might be safe to visit Arianrhod again. So he set out for her castle at Caer Sidi taking the boy with him. At first Arianrhod welcomed them. The boy looked on her with awe, thinking he had never seen a woman so beautiful and so stern. Then Arianrhod asked who the boy was.

'This young lad?' exclaimed Gwydion, 'Why, surely you know that he is your son!'

Then Arianrhod turned on him a face white with fury, while the sharp memory of her shame and betrayal rose up and filled her with bitterness.

'How dare you come here', she said, 'only to bring me further pain and dishonour!'

'What dishonour do I bring you,' said Gwydion, 'other than that of bringing up such a fine boy as this?'

She turned away abruptly and was silent for a long time, wrestling with herself.

'What is the name of the boy you say is mine?' she asked finally.

'He has not yet been given a name,' said Gwydion.

'Then,' she said, her face now burning red: 'I lay this fate upon him. He shall receive no name unless it comes from me. And I swear by all the gods that I shall never name him!'

Gwydion took a step back, 'By all that breathes, you are a wicked woman!' he cried. 'I know why you are angry – it is because you have lost the name of virgin! But the boy *shall* have a name, however much you plot against him!'

Angered beyond measure, Arianrhod swept from the room and immured herself in her inner chamber, so that Gwydion was obliged to leave with the young boy following, bewildered and sad.

Nevertheless, Gwydion did not return home, but lingered on the shore of the island deep in thought. Then he took some seaweed and dry sedge and, using his powers of transformation, turned them into a boat. Then he took more and turned it into skins of Cordovan leather. Lastly, he furnished the boat with a sail and he and the boy got in it and sailed round to the bay below the castle. There he changed their appearances so that they seemed like an elderly cobbler and his apprentice, and he began stitching the fine leather into shoes.

When Arianrhod looked out from her castle and saw them, she sent messengers down with details of her foot measurements and ordered them to make her some shoes. The next day the most exquisite leather shoes were sent up to her with fine gold patterns, but when she tried them on she found they were too big. So she sent again, but this time they were too small. At last, at Gwydion's request, she agreed to go in person to have her feet measured. She went down to where the boat was moored and saw the old man fashioning shoes and his boy stitching them. She greeted them but expressed surprise that one so skilled was unable to make the correct size for her.

'Although I have not yet succeeded,' said the man, 'Now I will!'

At this a little wren alighted on the deck of the boat and with great speed and accuracy the boy aimed a stone from his sling at it and caught it smack in the leg between sinew and bone. Arianrhod smiled,

'Truly,' she said, 'you have a sure hand, indeed.'

'Aha!' cried Gwydion, springing from the boat: 'Now he has a name, *Lleu Llaw Gyffes*, "He of the Sure Hand!"'

Immediately both boat and sail disappeared, as did the leather, and the disguise fell from the man so that she knew him as her brother. Then Arianrhod cried aloud: 'You will not get away with this evil you have done to me!'

Gwydion transformed the boy back to his own likeness and replied quietly, 'I have done you no evil as yet.'

'No?' retorted Arianrhod, 'Then I will lay a further fate upon the boy. He shall never obtain arms until I myself give them to him. And that I will never do!'

Then she turned away in great rage and took refuge in her castle. But Gwydion looked up at the waning sun and raised his fist to the skies.

'By the great Heavens,' he said, 'let her curse as she must, but the boy *will* have arms!'

After that a few more years passed in which Gwydion set about training Lleu in horsemanship and building up his athletic strength until he had the physique of a young man and was able to ride any horse in the land. Yet he still had no horse and arms of his own. So they set out again for Arianrhod's castle, this time passing themselves off as bards. Arianrhod gave them a great welcome and feasted them well. Then she asked the older bard for a tale. Gwydion, being skilled in the art, entertained the company late into the night. But after they retired he crept out alone and went into the woods. There he worked fast with herbs and the bones of birds, so that as dawn appeared, with it arose the illusion of a vast fleet of ships covering the seas around the island.

All in the castle awoke to the uproar of trumpets and shouting. When she saw the cause of it, Arianrhod ran to their chamber and began knocking desperately on the door.

'Help!' she cried. 'We are surrounded by enemy ships. There are so many it is impossible to see the ocean between them!'

'Yes, we heard trumpets and shouting,' said Gwydion, opening the door to her.

'Please,' said Arianrhod, wringing her hands, 'we have so few men here. What can we do?'

'Well, lady,' Gwydion replied, 'I advise you to close up the castle and we will help you defend it.'

'The gods be merciful to you!' said Arianrhod.

Then, as the sound of men approaching grew louder, she went and collected suits of armour for them.

'Lady,' said Gwydion, 'quickly help the boy to arm and I shall arm myself!'

'I shall indeed,' cried Arianrhod and in no time at all she had the boy armed.

'Now,' said Gwydion 'take off his armour for we no longer need it!'

At this a look of horror came over Arianrhod and she watched helplessly as the two young bards turned into the forms of Gwydion and Lleu and the sounds of the approaching fleet faded away.

'And now he is armed,' declared Gwydion 'with no thanks to you!'

'By all the gods,' she cried, 'you are an evil man, if you think you can outwit me. But you never shall! For I give my oath that the boy shall never take a mortal wife all the days of his life!'

'You may curse away, you wicked woman,' cried Gwydion, 'but he *shall* have a wife!'

When he returned to court again with Lleu, Gwydion went to Math and complained bitterly about Arianrhod's curse. The two men debated together and then Math said he had an idea of how they might outwit her. It was difficult to achieve, he said, and they would need to combine their powers, but he thought it would be possible. Greatly excited, Gwydion asked Math to reveal his plan.

COMMENTARY

Gods and magicians

Many of the characters in this story can be seen as euhemerized deities (see page 1). Math, in particular, has many features that identify him as a god. Although depicted as a ruler, he has the ability to hear speech from long distances. This ability, like that of the Irish hero Finn mac Cumhail, who can see over vast distances when he puts his thumb in his mouth, demonstrates intuitive and Otherworldly powers. Math is therefore both king and seer. As seer, he is aligned with cosmic forces. This is suggested by his supernatural ability being brought to him on the wind. As king, he is aligned with his kingdom and confined by his duty to it. This is symbolized by the prohibition which constrains him to rest his feet in the lap of a virgin. It is also because his magical power has to be insulated from the land itself (see page 95).

Lleu is also thought to be a deity. His name is similar to that of *Lugh*, the Irish god of light who is connected with the sun and kingship. He is also typical of the magical or divine child, for the story of his begetting and childhood contains all the hallmarks of the unknown boy king and can be compared to that of King Arthur. Lleu's mother is tricked into giving birth to him, his paternity is uncertain, he develops at a prodigious rate, and he is raised by foster-parents and taught by a magician. Coming of age, he recognizes his own royal identity and proves himself in military skill, after which he becomes king.

Gwydion is the Merlin figure in the story who uses his trickster-magician powers to engender the child king. He may even be the boy's father himself. His apparent punishment by Math involves him in shape-shifting with his brother into different animals and also different sexes. Such experience amounts to a training in shamanism, which was akin to that undergone by Ovates, the order of bardic seers. Shamanism involved the ability to cross barriers, such as between the human and animal worlds so that the initiate was able to access a particular animal's powers. It also involved crossing temporal and spiritual boundaries and was therefore linked with the Celtic idea of the reincarnation of the soul. During such training, the initiate was sometimes obliged to use cunning or trickery to obtain new knowledge.

Gwydion's theft of Pryderi's pigs can also be viewed as initiatory. The pigs had been given to him by Arawn. In Welsh myths Arawn was lord of the Underworld and pigs were especially associated with the Underworld as totem animals. They were therefore considered magical and were sometimes also allied with the feminine – the goddess Ceridwen's totem animal, for example, being a boar. Gwydion's stealing of the pigs can therefore be seen as a raid of the Underworld for its magical treasure. As an aspect of bardic spiritual training, we can understand it in psychological terms as seeking new understanding from the unconscious.

The Triple Goddess

Arianrhod is also a euhemerized deity. Her name means Silver Wheel and refers to the moon. She rules over Caer Sidi, a castle that contains the *awen* or seat of poetic inspiration. The castle is surrounded by three rings of fire and either one or three fountains. Caer Sidi, on its island, is therefore a type of Otherworld, for it contains the Fountain of Knowledge. Added to this, the Seat of Poetic Inspiration represents the ultimate in bardic insight, understanding and power. Arianrhod is both an Otherworldly guardian and a goddess. It is in this light that she views her state of virginity.

In ancient Celtic understanding, the virgin was one of the triple aspects of the great Celtic Goddess, the other two being mother and crone. These three aspects corresponded to three phases of the moon, the new white moon, the full red moon and the black empty moon. Like the moon, too, the Goddess was perpetually renewing herself. Turning like the seasons, she became spring, summer and winter and then spring again. As Earth Mother she was connected with the land and with the sovereignty of the land. It is important to understand her changing state and the fact that she had both a dark and a light face. The ancient Celts therefore regarded virginity as a renewable attribute of female divinity. It was not the limited understanding we have of the term today. However, because Arianrhod is misunderstood, the story reflects a conflict between old and new thinking. The ancient understanding also linked the Goddess as Sovereign of the Land with the King (page 47). Thus Math, as the good ruler, was in constant touch with the land, symbolized by the virgin.

The Dark Goddess

In this half of the story the Goddess is represented by two women whose roles overlap and who both claim virgin status. Although Goewin is the one who is raped, it is Arianrhod who gives birth. At the beginning of the story the fair face of the Goddess is prominent until she is wronged. Then in Arianrhod the two aspects are seen, first the fair one that welcomes her brother and that responds to the king's call for a new representative of the sovereignty of the land, and then the dark one, which becomes prominent after the birth of Lleu. In Celtic myths the Dark Goddess, sometimes known as the *Cailleach*, or hag, is the Challenger. In this guise she sets tests for the hero. But after the challenges have been met, she gives rewards either of kingship or, like the Loathly Lady who tests Gawain in the Arthurian legends, the bride, or beautiful Feminine. Often the bride and the kingdom go together. The nature of the three curses that Arianrhod lays on Lleu strongly suggests they are tests of kingship.

The three tests

Although Gwydion teaches Lleu all he can, there are vital parts of his training that he needs to learn from the Realm of the Feminine. The first of these is to discover his name, which really means to discover his identity. This is why Lleu shoots the wren with his sling in front of Arianrhod. Wren hunting was a strong Celtic custom. A story went that in a contest for leadership among the birds, the wren had outwitted the eagle by riding on its back while it soared higher and higher and had finally fluttered above it, taking the title of King of the Birds. The ritual of the killing of the wren at the time of the winter solstice was therefore practised by the Celts as a symbol of the annual sacrifice of the king. By shooting the wren, Lleu demonstrated knowledge of his own royal identity and could therefore claim his name from Arianrhod.

The second test involved being armed. Arianrhod's role in this is reminiscent of the roles of Celtic women in training warriors in military skills. The most famous of these was *Scathach* who trained the great Irish hero Cuchulainn. Another example is the band of nine hags who give military training in *Peredur*, another tale from the *Mabinogion*. The role of the Dark Goddess as Challenger evidently included testing military prowess. Therefore, only after Lleu has learned feats of arms from Gwydion and demonstrated his boldness in the face of a vast enemy, is Arianrhod able to give him his arms.

The third test is for the king to find and win his destined female consort. In apparently denying him human love, Arianrhod is saying that, as king, he cannot marry a mortal woman because his ritual destiny requires a more symbolic union. (See Part II (Chapter 9).)

The Goddess discredited

The Fourth Branch of the *Mabinogion* is thought to be later than the other three. If that is the case it may reflect a changing attitude in belief. Although the ancient Celts venerated the Great Goddess and respected her dark side as an important aspect of nature, in this myth she seems to be misunderstood or perhaps deliberately discredited. The rape of Goewin and the shaming of Arianrhod demonstrate a dishonouring of the Goddess's powers. Also the depiction of Arianrhod as a purely vengeful sorceress and, in Part II, of the Earth Goddess as a heartless murderess, again reveals a misunderstanding and blackening of their roles. A moral dimension has entered which is at odds with the old understanding. This could indicate the turning point between the matriarchal and patriarchal perspective, a possibility which must be borne in mind when seeking an understanding of this myth.

9 | MATH, SON OF MATHONWY, PART II: THE FLOWER BRIDE

Math sent servants to collect branches and blossoms of the oak, the broom and the meadowsweet. All the while he and Gwydion were preparing the inner chamber, purifying it with herbs, marking it with *ogham* symbols and filling it with incense smoke. Then the lengthy spells began. Muttering and chanting for hour upon hour they built her, limbs out of saplings, hands out of leaves, fresh and green veined, skin out of blossoms and hair out of silken strands of stalk. At first she was like some tree-web, her arms stiff, her fingers spiked. Still they worked, softening her, breathing into her, whispering the words of enchantment.

When their work was done Math spoke the final words of power. At first nothing happened, they gazed at their blossom-covered beauty and saw only the foliage of spring. Then, slowly, as they continued to gaze, strands of silver energy began running from head to arm, from arm to hand, from belly to knee, from knee to toe. Then with a sudden convulsion like the shivering of wind in a tree, the flower-form threw back her head and laughed. The sound of her laughter was like the trickling of a stream on the mountain, pure and clear. Then she clapped her hands and bark and leaf pieces fell in a cloud around her. She stepped unsteadily forward, and there she was alive, smooth limbed, with petal-soft skin and dew-bright eyes.

They called her Blodeuwedd, which means 'created from flowers,' and gave her a baptism according to the rites of that time. She was the rarest beauty a man ever saw and when she was presented to Lleu he wept at his good fortune. A great wedding feast was held and Lleu wanted to give his bride the whole world and everything in it.

'It is hard for a man to maintain himself without possessions', said Gwydion, guessing his thoughts.

'Then I will give him my best cantrev,' said Math, and he bestowed on him the Cantrev of Dinodig, later called Ardudwy, which had a fine palace. There the couple lived and Lleu reigned over that part of the land and was well loved by his people.

One day Lleu set out to visit Math at Caer Dathal leaving Blodeuwedd behind. Blodeuwedd walked about the court alone, feeling restless. Suddenly she heard the sound of a horn and, looking out at the woodland, saw an exhausted stag break through into a clearing with a crowd of dogs and huntsmen after it. After that came a crowd of men pursuing on foot. Then she saw the chief huntsman spur ahead of the others in a bid to come up with the stag. He pursued it as far as the River Cynvael, where at last he overtook and killed it. He had barely finished flaying the carcass when night fell. Seeing the gates of the palace so near, he came towards them, seeking hospitality. Blodeuwedd told her servants to invite him in, saying, 'This chief will speak ill of us if we force him to go into another land at this late hour.'

So Gronwy Pebyr, Lord of Penllyn, entered the palace at Blodeuwedd's bidding and was invited to dine with her. As soon as Blodeuwedd looked at him she was filled with a violent passion for him and he for her, so that they were forced to confess their love for each other that very evening. Blodeuwedd took him secretly to her chamber that night and the next morning she begged him not to go. He stayed a further night and the following day they were desperate to find a way to be together.

'There is nothing to be done', said Gronwy, 'unless you find out how Lleu can be killed. You can do it by pretending to care about him. Promise me you will.'

Blodeuwedd promised and Gronwy took his leave.

When Lleu returned, Blodeuwedd greeted him lovingly. But that night she went silent and refused to speak to him.

'What's the matter?' he asked, 'Are you ill?'

'No,' she replied. 'You will think it foolish, but I can't stop worrying about your death, I'm afraid you might die before I do.'

'The gods reward you,' he replied, laughing, ' but unless it is my fate, I cannot easily be killed.'

'Then tell me how it can be done,' she said. 'That will stop me worrying.'

So Lleu, believing in her love for him, told her of the spell Gwydion had put on him while he was being formed in the oak chest. It prevented his being killed either on horseback or on foot, either indoors or outdoors, either on water or dry land.

Blodeuwedd was in despair.

'Then how *can* you be killed?' she asked.

'Well,' said Lleu, 'only if a cauldron of water is set beside a river and a thatched roof is created over half of it and a goat is brought and steadied beside the cauldron. Then if I climb up and place one foot on the goat's back and the other on the cauldron, I am neither on water or on dry land, neither inside nor outside, neither on horseback nor on foot.'

'And is that how you can be killed?' asked Blodeuwedd.

'No,' Lleu replied. 'Only if after that a spear that has been forged for a year during religious rituals is aimed at me.'

Then Blodeuwedd sent a message to Gronwy, who immediately began honing a spear at the prescribed times.

A year later Blodeuwedd prepared the cauldron and the thatched roof by the river and had the goat tethered and waiting. Then she ran and called Lleu.

'Come and see what I have prepared for you,' she said. 'I should love to see you try to balance on the goat and the cauldron.'

Then, dancing and clapping her hands, she persuaded him to take part in the game. So, after several attempts and much laughter, Lleu eventually managed to steady himself on the goat and the side of the cauldron.

But as he raised himself up, a shadow moved on the hillside above and a high note whistled through the air as a spear came hurtling towards him. Before he could move, it had struck into his side. Lleu let out a terrifying scream but immediately his body changed into the form of an eagle, which flew stiffly into the sky with the arrow shaft sticking out of it.

After Lleu's disappearance, Gronwy took charge of his lands, adding them to his own, and moved into Lleu's palace with Blodeuwedd. When news of Lleu's disappearance reached Gwydion, he set out immediately to look for him. He travelled the land seeking his nephew, but was unable to find him. Then one day he knocked at the door of a farmhouse in Arvon and asked for a bed for the night. That evening the farmer and his young swineherd were talking about the strange behaviour of one of the sows. It seemed that every day as soon as she was let out of her sty, she charged off faster than the youth could keep up with her and disappeared. Every night she returned, but where she had been all day remained a mystery. Gwydion offered to try to find out himself. So, early the next morning the sow was let out and she charged off with Gwydion after her. She rushed down the valley, forded a river, crossed some fields and then bolted across a brook. Gwydion kept up with her until, at last, coming into another valley she stopped under a large tree and began feeding greedily on rotting flesh.

Then Gwydion looked up into the tree and saw that at its very top was an eagle which fluttered from time to time shaking itself and letting its wounded flesh drop down to the ground. When Gwydion guessed who the eagle was he wept for a while and then went deeply into himself and at last began to sing an *englyn*:

Grows an oak between two lakes
Darkly shadowed sky and glen.
If I do not speak untruth
These are petals from Lleu's fair flowers.

Then he paused and watched as the eagle slowly and with great difficulty descended to the centre of the tree where it settled again. Then Gwydion sang another *englyn*:

Grows an oak on upland plain,
nor rain wets it nor heat melts.
Nine score hardships hath it felt,
on its branch, Lleu Llaw Gyffes.

Gwydion paused again, watching as the eagle slowly descended to the lowest branch. Then he sang a third *englyn*:

Grows an oak upon a steep,
sanctuary of a fine fair lord.
If I do not speak untruth
Lleu will come into my lap.

At this the eagle came down upon Gwydion's knee and Gwydion struck him with his wand, returning him to human form. But Lleu was in a piteous state, little more than skin and bone. So Gwydion carried him back to Math and for a year he was tended by the most skilled physicians in the land until he was completely healed.

After this Lleu felt it was time for retribution and the restoration of his kingdom. He consulted with Math and they called together the whole of Gwynedd and set out for Lleu's old palace, Lleu himself going on ahead.

When word reached Blodeuwedd that he was coming, she fled to the mountains with her maidens who, fearing his pursuit, looked backwards as they ran. They fell in a lake and were drowned, leaving Blodeuwedd to run on alone. Lleu caught up with her, seizing her arm and twisting her round so that he could look once more on her beautiful face. He held her there while she panted and struggled. At last he said, 'I will not kill you.'

Blodeuwedd felt herself relax for a moment while a faint hope washed through her and she reached towards him.

'But I will do that which is worse,' he said. 'Because of the shame you have brought upon me you must never show your face in the light of day. So I will make you a bird, one that is feared and attacked by other birds and that only flies at night. You shall become an owl.'

As soon as he said this, her mouth, which was poised to kiss him, hardened and sharpened, her eyes rounded and yellowed and her skin shivered into feathers. She spread silver-grey wings and lifted herself shrieking into the sky.

Meanwhile Gronwy withdrew into his kingdom of Penllyn and sent an embassy to Lleu offering him lands, gold, silver or any other prize as redress for the injury he had received. But Lleu refused all offers demanding instead that Gronwy should stand where he had stood when he was killed so that he, in turn, could stand where Gronwy had stood and cast a spear at him. Then Gronwy asked his family and courtiers whether any of them would volunteer to take the blow for him, but they all refused. So Gronwy set out himself and arrived at the place by the river where Lleu had stood. At the last moment he begged Lleu to let him put a stone between himself and the blow, arguing that it was a woman's wiles that had caused the trouble in the first place. Lleu allowed this but it did him no good. The spear flung by Lleu passed right through the stone and through Gronwy's body with such force that it came out at the other side. And even today there stands a stone on the bank of the river Cynvael with a hole in it, named *Llech Gronwy* or Gronwy's Stone.

Then Lleu ruled over his lands and, in time, became Lord over the whole of Gwynedd.

COMMENTARY

The continuing cycle

In the second half of the myth, Lleu's magical destiny continues. He becomes King, marries a beautiful woman and is betrayed by her. This betrayal leads him to undergo a form of death after which he is returned to life to re-establish his rule.

But the apparently faithless Blodeuwedd is none other than the Earth Goddess herself and the third of the trilogy of women in the myth. As king, it was Lleu's destiny to wed the land. The image of a woman created out of nature is therefore a compelling and vivid depiction of the Earth Goddess. Because she represents an impersonal force, she appears immoral from a human perspective, but it is her role to push the cycle on towards the ritual death of her king and consort. In this respect Gronwy Pebyr (Gronwy the Staunch) is the new ruler, who appears on the scene as a hunter. He is the one destined to fall under the spell of the Earth Goddess in order to kill and replace the old wren/king.

Kings and heroes were usually under some sort of magical protection as well as having specific *geasa* or prohibitions. The purpose of these may have been to make sure that their deaths could come about at the proper time. This would explain why Gwydion leaves a loophole in the special protective spell which he puts on Lleu. But, because Lleu is both an image of the sacrificial king and of his regeneration, instead of dying he shape-shifts into an eagle (the old king of the birds). After being restored to life, he punishes Blodeuwedd by turning her into an owl.

However, in this way, Lleu is completing her cycle and helping her become the Crone. For the owl symbolizes wisdom and the Crone is a type of Wise Old Woman.

Englyns

These were considered the most powerfully magical form of Welsh poetic utterance. For the secret of bardic power was ultimately poetic. The incantatory quality of rhyme, rhythm and metre was the essence of this and one reason why the bards kept their literature oral. The *englyns* are the most developed form of bardic power so far demonstrated by Gwydion. He uses them in his highest task, that of calling the soul back to life. Each verse is focused on an aspect of the great oak tree, which is one with the Tree of Life, known in Norse legend as *Yggdrasil*. The image of the tree with the dying king on it, speared in the side, is analogous to that of Christ.

Bardic initiation

In the same way as Lleu and Gwydion are bound together in the story, so too are the twin themes of kingly and bardic initiation. For Gwydion also seems to go through distinct stages of development. At the beginning, when he raids both Goewin's virtue and the Underworld (in the snatching of Pryderi's pigs), he appears like a shadow magician or trickster figure. After this he undergoes shamanistic training under the direction of Math. He also journeys three times to Arianrhod's palace on the Otherworldly island which contains the Poetic Seat of Inspiration. (The great poet-seer Taliesin speaks of having been 'three times in the prison of Arianrhod'.) It is therefore possible that Gwydion's visits to Arianrhod are an indication of bardic training.

At the end of the myth, Gwydion's shamanistic experience allows him to enter the lifeforce of the sow and go with her to find Lleu. Her feeding on carrion is indicative of her link with the Underworld. Symbolically this is where she has led Gwydion so that he can bring Lleu back from the dead. When Gwydion speaks the *englyns* and restores Lleu to life, he is exercising full druidic powers, having gained a deep understanding of the mysteries of life and death.

There were typically three grades of training for the Celtic visionary, that of the bard, the ovate (or seer) and the druid. In his skill at bardic storytelling, his shamanistic experience and his druidic command of the Otherworldly power of poetry, it is possible to trace Gwydion's progression through all three orders.

The Trickster

In this myth two powerful archetypal figures are typically paired. They are the king and the magician or trickster figure. As we have seen, the king is allied to the hero and like the hero is obliged to go on a journey of challenge and initiation. He must also undergo the fate of the wounded king who must be healed. But he cannot set out on the quest and he cannot heal himself without the help of the magician.

The role of the magician overlaps with that of the trickster or fool. Jung describes the trickster as a shapeshifter who is half-animal, half-divine. He is amoral, anarchistic and irreverent but, as such, provides access to the unruly forces which the good ruler by definition must exclude. His function is to keep the ruler in touch with the irrational, so that he can partake of its powers at the appropriate time. Being a shapeshifter and having undergone experiences of animal life as well as having performed feats of trickery and illusion, Gwydion exhibits some typical characteristics of the trickster. It is the trickster's curiosity that makes him embark on quests and that motivates the king to do so. Gwydion masterminds Lleu's journey and guides him through his initiation tests. Being a shapeshifter, he is also highly inventive and enjoys outwitting opponents in subtle and unusual ways. In this respect, too, Gwydion obviously relishes his contest with Arianrhod.

But, like Gwydion, the childish trickster can mature into the Wise Fool or Magician (otherwise he becomes stuck, like the Norse god, Loki, as a mere mischief-maker). This development is often prompted by love. By taking responsibility for Lleu, Gwydion is enabled to mature his art to the point where he is able to heal him. To do this he needs to command the magical powers found in the irrational which he has formerly used mostly in play. But, like the child, he has learned through play and become fearless of this realm. He is therefore equipped to handle its powers. Jung draws a parallel at this stage between the Fool and Christ, the Fool or shaman becoming a type of wounded saviour figure, because only the 'wounded wounder' can be the agent of healing.

By showing the intertwining of these two archetypal figures, the King and the Fool, in their separate initiatory quests, this myth holds the keys to the great secrets of inner wisdom. It is possible that the story evolved as a means of containing this wisdom in hidden form. Rites of initiation at that time were secretly guarded, being intended only for leader and shaman figures who undertook them on behalf of society. But some psychologists today believe that society has evolved to a stage where each individual is now being challenged to undertake his own journey. If this is the case, then an understanding of the role of myth in mapping the journey is crucial.

10 OISIN'S JOURNEY TO THE OTHERWORLD

This 'romance' tells the story of Oisin's 300-year stay in the Otherworld (the Land of Youth). The story is also known as 'The Last of the Fianna', since by the time Oisin returns to this world, that is what he has become. It is one of the Ossianic verses, many of which include dialogues between Oisin (Ossian) and St Patrick. It was probably first written down in the twelfth century and was recorded in *The Colloquy of the Ancients*. P. W. Joyce wrote in 1907 that there was a literal translation of it by Professor O'Looney in the Transactions of the Ossianic Society. Other versions vary in the details of the wonders of the Otherworld, and in the degree of danger associated with it and with the fairy maid.

Oisin's meeting with St Patrick at the end of the story may be a late addition to an earlier oral legend. Oisin is the son of Finn mac Cumhail, leader of the *Fianna* – the élite warrior band dating from around 400. Oisin probably did exist as a historical character, although he gradually became mythologized. St Patrick, by the same token, definitely existed. He came to Ireland in 432, and worked as a missionary there for around 60 years. However, the Ossianic verses in written form date mostly from the post-Viking era and we can guess that this story was probably recorded between 1043 and 1170.

Finn, the great hero and leader of the Fianna, had a son. This son was called Oisin – meaning 'Fawn' – and he was a hero in his own right, a leading member of the Fianna, as well as being a poet. Perhaps it was his poetic soul that led him into the Otherworld.

One day the Fianna were hunting the deer on the heather-clad shores of Loch Lene, in the mountains of Kerry. Presently Finn's extraordinarily acute hearing detected a sound: someone was approaching on a silver-shod horse. Soon the rider came into view out of a mist across the lake, a delicately featured woman riding high and upright on a magnificent white steed. She rode across the surface of the lake and the Fianna, all skilled horsemen, noted her skill and confidence – not to mention her ability to ride on water!

When the maiden rode up and reined in her horse, the men were struck dumb by her loveliness. Her bright eyes, cornflower blue, spoke of a land visited in dreams. Her golden hair, circled by a gold band, flowed onto her slim shoulders, which were covered by a silken cloak of rich brown starred with red gold. She walked her horse slowly up to Finn, who at last spoke.

'Tell us, princess – for that you must surely be – your name and that of your country, and what you want from us.'

'Great leader of the Fianna, I come from a land far off in the Western Sea, the Land of Youth. My father is indeed the king there and I am known as Niamh of the Golden Hair. I come to ask you for something.'

'If it is in my power, I will give it.'

'It is something of yours, but not in your power. I come because I have watched your son from afar and heard of his deeds and noble character. I have come because I love him and desire him for my husband.'

Next to Finn, wondering at these words, was Oisin. Finding a voice from within, he answered for himself: 'Princess, you are the fairest of all creatures. I believe I would choose you of all the women in the world.'

'In that case,' she answered quickly, 'you are now under *geis* to come with me to the Land of Youth. But have no fear. It is a land of unceasing delight, of treasures, honey and wine. The trees bear fragrant blossom and ripe fruit at one and the same time, and it is always summer. I'll give you a hundred well-forged swords, a hundred robes of satin and silk, a hundred prancing horses and a hundred eager hounds. You'll have armour that cannot be pierced and a sword that cannot miss its stroke. Warriors will attend you, sweet harpers and renowned poets will devote their arts to you.

Moreover, so long as you remain you will never grow old, but rather shall enjoy the full power and freshness of youth for ever.'

Oisin replied that he could not resist her even if he wanted to. At this, Finn and the Fianna gave three shouts of lamentation, for they feared never to see Oisin again in this world. Oisin himself was taken fully by the maiden's beauty and the lure of the land she promised, and at any rate he thought he could always return to visit his father and the Fianna.

Niamh made her horse stand next to Oisin's and Oisin, still wonder struck, climbed on behind her. She raised her small hand and with no further farewell the pair sped off. The white horse galloped effortlessly over the grey waves of the lake towards the west, moving as swiftly as a cloud shadow on a fresh March day. Soon the mist closed around them and they were lost to the men on the shore.

The pair rode on at an unvarying pace. Oisin had no idea of their course and from time to time he was distracted by strange sights appearing and disappearing in the mist. Palaces, mansions and summer houses emerged as if from a dream and were lost again before Oisin could fully focus on them. A fawn bounded over the waves, closely pursued by a white hound with red ears. A young woman holding a golden apple rode past pursued closely by a young man whose yellow silk cloak billowed out after him. When Oisin asked Niamh about these things she told him to ignore them, as they were nothing compared to the wonders he was soon to see.

The mist gradually cleared, but after a while it grew dark and a storm arose. Distant rumblings turned to loud thunderclaps, the wind churned up the sea beneath them and lightning lit up the sky. The white horse, undaunted, continued at a steady pace and although the rain pelted down, Oisin and Niamh remained dry. Before long the storm passed and the sun shone. Now Oisin saw that they were fast approaching a country lovely to behold. As they drew near, he saw level plains, blue hills, lakes and waterfalls. Out of the landscape grew a splendid palace, beautifully ornate, perfectly proportioned and dazzlingly bejewelled.

'This', announced Niamh of the Golden Hair, 'is the Land of Youth. Here you will find all the wonders I promised and more.'

The horse slowed and halted and the pair got down. A troop of noble warriors approached, brightly dressed and eager to escort the princess and Oisin. A procession of joyful men and women courtiers followed them, headed by a king whose great dignity Oisin could discern, even from afar. The queen came after, attended by lovely maidens. It seemed to Oisin, who had seen many wonders, that nowhere could there be a more wonderful and glittering gathering.

Oisin was welcomed royally, bathed and dressed in fine clothes as befitted a prince. A banquet was prepared and after ten days of feasting, with the most diverting entertainments imaginable and wonders that Oisin could hardly believe, he was at last married to Niamh. He was in no way disappointed by his new wife, by their palaces and lands or by the ever-smiling welcome of the people there.

Life for Oisin went on like this for what seemed to be three years, although since it was always summer it was hard to be sure. If anything he felt younger and fitter as the days passed and his wife appeared – although it seemed impossible – even more beautiful. Yet there grew in Oisin a tiny seed of discontent. At first it was too small to notice. Then occasionally it was as if a wisp of cloud had passed over the sun for a moment. Then one day he woke from a dream and found that he missed his father, the Fianna, and the land of Ireland.

'I want to visit my homeland,' he told Niamh. She sighed, but without surprise, as she had long seen the desire growing in Oisin.

'Very well. You may go, though it grieves me for I fear that you will not return. Take my white horse, for he knows the way. However, listen to me well, dear husband. You will find things changed in Ireland now, but whatever you do, do not dismount. If you do and your feet once more touch the soil of your homeland, you will never be able to return and you will never see me again.'

With some misgiving, yet still with a powerful longing for his home and his old companions, Oisin mounted the great white horse and set off. He rode through the mist across the sea, heading ever eastwards, until he saw the shores of green Ireland appearing at last. Yet his gladness and excitement left him as he perceived the change that had indeed taken place. It was as if a glory had passed away, leaving everything grey and lacklustre. As he rode through the land he saw no proud warriors and no Fianna. The people he passed were small and puny and laboured with difficulty under even the smallest loads. When they looked up, they seemed amazed to see Oisin.

Seeing an old man by the road, Oisin stopped and asked him for news of Finn and the Fianna. 'The Fianna?' repeated the old man, puzzled. 'There are old stories of a hero called Finn who led a band by that name, but they're all long gone.'

Oisin thanked the man and rode on in shock and sadness until he came to a field where some of the little men were straining to move a boulder and were in danger of being crushed by it. Oisin for a moment forgot his sorrows and rode to their aid. Leaning from his saddle he easily shifted the boulder and – to the men's astonishment – sent it bounding across the field. But as he leaned over, the strain told on the golden saddle girth and it snapped suddenly, pitching him onto the ground. The white horse shook himself and took off towards the west. Oisin, for his part had little time to appreciate his homeland. All his senses began to fade and he found himself weakened and bowed as if under a great burden. And indeed he was: it was the burden of the three centuries that had in fact passed since his departure. They fell upon him like winter snows and before the astonished eyes of the watching men he became, in moments, ancient, stooped and white-haired.

The men overcame their shock and fear and helped the old man from the field and into a hut. One of them ran to fetch a holy father, Patrick, who came and listened with keen interest to Oisin's incredible tale. Some say that Patrick converted the old man to the new faith. Others report that when Patrick said Finn was now in hell, Oisin scornfully swore that he would rather be in hell with the *Fianna* than in heaven without them, adding: 'Great, then, would be the shame for God not to release Finn from the shackles of pain; for if God Himself were in bonds my chief would fight on his behalf.'

COMMENTARY

The Otherworld

Vital to an understanding of this story is the nature of the Otherworld and what it meant to the Celts, as well as what it means in modern psychological terms. Celtic mythology contains many stories in which men journey into the mysterious Otherworld, usually to marry fairy women, or at least to enjoy their favours. These women are referred to in Irish Gaelic as *bean-sidhe* or banshees. The latter Anglicized term has taken on pejorative connotations, but the character of these women in the early tales is magical, mysterious and wonderful, although with a hint of danger which stems from their irresistibility and from the difficulty of returning from their world to this one.

In some of these tales there is a stronger element of seduction involved. For example in the tale of Connla of the Golden Hair and the Fairy Maiden, the maiden falls in love with Connla and tries to tempt him away from his fathers's side. Interestingly, she is invisible to all but Connla. On this occasion the chanting of the Druid Coran is sufficient to protect the young man. However, as the maiden leaves she throws Connla an apple – which often represents the delights of the Otherworld – and for the next month he will eat nothing else. (One is reminded of Oisin's fleeting glimpse of a youth pursuing a maiden with a golden apple.) When the maiden returns, although Connla feels some reluctance to leave his native land, he nevertheless feels compelled to go with her.

Oisin seems to have more choice than Connla. Yet he decides very quickly to go with Niamh, apparently persuaded by her beauty and by her account of the wonderful land to which she will take him – even though he has a son, Oscar, and probably a wife too. Niamh is too attractive a proposition to resist, and even if Oisin is deluded, Finn and the Fianna seem to have a stronger grasp of reality: hence their lamentation.

Strangely, in one lesser-known version of the story, Niamh is rather less attractive at first, as a druid has enchanted her to have the head of a pig until she marries! In a gender reversal of other tales in which a goddess at first appears in her hag aspect, Oisin nobly recognizes Niamh's hidden divinity and agrees to marry her.

One interpretation of the Otherworld journey is that it represents a shamanistic passage into the spirit world. It may also be about soul loss or about possession by an archetype. The familiar image of the man who finds the woman irresistible is, in Jungian terms, projecting his anima (variously seen as the soul and the inner feminine) onto the woman. He is filled with longing because he perceives an essential part of himself as being 'out there', in the woman. In different terms, what he perceives is the archetype of the goddess, offering the ultimate in comfort and sexual delight, a union with the very source of life. This is a tall order for the ordinary woman expected to carry the projection!

The conflict that these myths attempt to resolve is that of being drawn to the spirit world, yet having to live in this one. Hence the ambivalence towards the Otherworld that one finds in Celtic myths, with the sense of danger that lies behind the glittering splendour. Characteristically the hero must enter a realm of the unconscious, surrendering the control normally guaranteed by the conscious mind and the ego. Hence the Otherworld is often reached over, or through, water, a symbol of the unconscious. For Oisin it lies across a sea obscured by mist. In the Irish story of Loegaire going to help a fairy man retrieve his abducted wife, Loegaire and his men reach the Otherworld by diving into a lake. In a Blackfoot story the hero dives into a lake to fetch the tribe's first horses from a similar spirit world. There are also folktales and stories in other mythologies of water sprites or mermaids taking men down to their land beneath the water.

It is significant in Oisin's story that he has to climb onto Niamh's horse, riding behind her, with her hands firmly clasping his. Moreover, when he asks her about the strange sights that emerge from the mist like dream images, she declines to tell him what they are. In fact, she has almost all the power in the relationship, except in that she appears to need a mortal husband. Niamh's power, however, is not sufficient to keep Oisin in the Land of Youth against his will. When he begins to miss his homeland and the Fianna, she has to let him go. Naively he thinks that he will be able to visit and then go back to her.

We should also comment on what life is like in Oisin's Otherworld. It sounds wonderful, an endless round of untarnished delights. From other stories, we know that there are battles there too: Cuchulainn is asked to fight in one, the story of the Gilla Dacka contains details of Otherworldly strife, and Oisin would have no need of a sword or warrior attendants if the Otherworld were entirely peaceful. Yet one gets the impression that war exists there only because to the Celts a world with no opportunity for personal glory in battle would be unappealing – or simply too hard to imagine. On the whole, the Otherworld offers a life of perpetual ease, but one in which there is no challenge and therefore no purpose. This is the subtler danger of the Otherworld: it might make the hero like the lotus eaters in Homer's *Odyssey*, passive and unmotivated.

The passing of time

The disparity between time in this world and the Otherworld is a feature that appears elsewhere in Celtic myths and it is interesting to compare this with some modern scientific ideas. Einstein established that time passes more and more slowly, relative to a fixed point, as one travels faster. An astronaut making a 20-year space voyage at 99.9 per cent of the speed of light would return to find that 10,000 years had passed on earth. This means that in theory a kind of time-travel into the future, which is the direction in which Oisin travels, could take place.

Otherworldly time-travel stories could hint at some collectively unconscious insight into these ideas or be saying something about our subjective experience of time. They could also be attempts to convey an idea of eternity – which, as Joseph Campbell points out, is not just 'for ever', but an experience of being completely outside time. Lastly, they may reflect the shaman's experience in journeying into the unconscious.

Coming down to earth

When Oisin reaches Ireland, he is shocked to see that everything has faded and that men have become puny. This could point to the fact that if one has an Otherworldly experience, when one returns to the normal world, once again perceived at a distance, through the filter of the ego, and in time – then it may seem dull by comparison. This of course would be another reason for regarding the Otherworld as a dangerous place to visit: it spoils you for normal life. One thinks of Wordsworth's regret, reflecting on the child's unclouded perception: 'That there hath past away a glory from the earth.'

In the version of the story given here, Oisin falls to earth ('comes down to earth with a bang') when his saddle girth breaks. This seems to symbolize a breaking of the ties with Niamh and her world: he 'snaps out of it'. In another version Oisin removes a boulder to uncover the horn used to summon the Fianna – and perhaps, symbolically, to impart his newfound Otherworldly knowledge. In his eagerness to sound the horn he touches the earth with one foot.

Joseph Campbell notes that Oisin has gone into the subliminal experience fully awake and has incorporated the timeless state into his personality, so that when he returns, as the hero must, the danger for him is all the greater. He is wrenched out of eternity and into the realm of time. His spirit is pulled away from the centre. As Campbell puts it: 'The balance of perfection is lost, the spirit falters, and the hero falls.'

The small stature of the men whom Oisin encounters on his return, which makes him a giant by comparison, is echoed in the myths of other cultures, which suggest that there was once a Golden Age in which human beings were either physically bigger or more noble and more heroic. The author of Genesis tells us of early Hebrews living for hundreds of years, and about the Nephilim, 'the sons of God ... the mighty men that were of old, the men of renown'. Similarly, a Hindu myth tells of a great and noble warrior king, Muchukunda, whom the gods reward with endless sleep in a cave. When eventually awoken, like Oisin he is surprised to find that men have shrunk, which causes him to retire to a life of spiritual contemplation; the equivalent for Oisin is to investigate Christianity – and either to embrace or reject it, depending on which version of his story one reads.

The horse as insulation

Niamh first appears on horseback and does not dismount; instead she gets Oisin to climb on behind her. When Oisin returns he is safe as long as he remains on horseback, symbolically insulated from the temporal world. This idea that bearers of spiritual power must be protected from the dispersal of their power by their touching the ground is widespread in myth and custom. The Welsh ruler and mage Math Mathonwy (see page 63) must have his feet in the lap of a virgin, except when going to war (when presumably he would be on horseback); the Aztec emperor Montezuma was always carried on the shoulders of his nobles; in some Native American tribes the eldest son is traditionally kept from direct contact with the earth as a child.

Sir James G. Frazer comments in *The Golden Bough*:

Apparently holiness, magical virtue, taboo, or whatever we may call that mysterious quality which is supposed to pervade sacred or tabooed persons … can be discharged and drained away by contact with the earth, which on this theory serves as an excellent conductor for the magical fluid.

Customs observed in many parts of the world suggest that this need to insulate the bearer of power is also the origin of the traditional 'red carpet' rolled out for royalty, especially when a royal personage first sets foot in a country.

Paganism and Christianity

Oisin's meeting with Patrick is interesting for its attempt to draw together two worlds, the pagan and the Christian. It seems there was relatively little animosity between Christianity and the native paganism in Ireland. Witness the fact that the Christian monks recorded so many of the pagan myths and with so little alteration (as far as we can tell). In South America, by comparison, the Spanish church made every effort to wipe out Mayan myths. Yet the Oisin–Patrick legend still points to a need to make peace between the two sets of beliefs.

11 THE VOYAGE OF MAELDUN

The oldest copy of this tale is in the Book of the Dun Cow. This copy is mutilated, but others are in the Yellow Book of Lecan and in the British Museum. The story itself may date from about 700 or, in oral form, much earlier, although the 'plunderers' mentioned are almost certainly Vikings, who did not arrive in Ireland until the end of the eighth century. This detail may have been added to the original. In addition, the strongly Christian ending may have been added at any time after Christianity came to Ireland in the middle of the fifth century: this ending does feel as though it has been superimposed on an earlier pagan version. It may even be a reworking by the twelfth-century copyist. The present version is based on one translated by P. W. Joyce for his *Old Celtic Romances* (1907).

There was once a widely respected chief named Allil Ocar Aga, Lord of the Owenaght tribe. One day a fleet of plunderers landed unexpectedly on his territory and overran it. Allil sought refuge in the church, but the attackers were heathens who had no respect for God, so they murdered him and burned the church over his body. Shortly after this, a son was born to Allil's widow. She called him Maeldun, 'Chief of the Fort'. Wishing to conceal his birth and wanting the boy to have a father, she gave him to the king and queen of that country to bring up. He was a fine boy, much loved by all who came into contact with him, and he grew up happily with his three foster-brothers, believing their father and mother to be his own.

When Maeldun grew to be a young man, he excelled in sports, in chess and in all manly pursuits. Then one day a jealous young noble confronted him: 'Maeldun, it is the source of much shame to us that we must yield to a youth of unknown parentage.' Maeldun was bewildered, then dismayed. He went straight to the Queen and asked her the meaning of the young man's claim. Reluctantly she took him to his real mother, who with equal reluctance revealed to him the identity of his father.

Knowing himself now to be the son of Allil, Maeldun set out for his father's territory, accompanied by his three foster-brothers, all noble and handsome youths like himself. When they arrived and Maeldun revealed himself to be the son of Allil, the people there welcomed him and treated him with respect and generosity, so that he soon forgot the resentment he had recently encountered.

Some time later, Maeldun was passing the time with a number of other young men. Their game was to cast stones over the roof of the church, still charred from the attack of the plunderers. Seeing Maeldun cheerfully taking part, a bitter-tongued servant named Bricka admonished him:

'It would be more honourable for you to avenge the man who was burned to death here than to entertain yourself hurling stones over his blackened bones.'

'Who was he, and who slew him?' asked Maeldun.

'He was Allil Ocar Aga, your father, slain by plunderers. What's more, the same men are still sailing in the same fleet.'

Maeldun was distressed to hear this. He dropped his stone, cast his cloak around him and went asking after the whereabouts of these plunderers. He could gain no information until eventually he learned that the fleet was far off and could only be reached by sea. Resolving to mount an expedition to seek revenge, he visited the Druid Nuca to seek advice. The old man told him when to start building his boat and when to set sail, and that he should take with him a crew of 60 men, no more, no less.

Maeldun set about building a large, triple-hide boat – a curragh, with a sail and oars. He did this following all the druid's instructions, and he chose his crew of 60 men, including his two friends Germane and Diuran. The curragh set to sea on the correct day, with the people gathered on the shore waving goodbye and good luck. Most of those watching were related to someone on board and there was trepidation as well as excitement in the air. The men onshore helped to launch the craft, and their cheers as it settled in the water mingled with the cry of the seabirds.

The crew dipped their oars and began to pull, but when the curragh was still only a little way from the land, there was a commotion in the crowd, and it parted to let through three determined young men. These were Maeldun's three foster-brothers, and they shouted and gestured to him to come back and let them on board to join the expedition.

'We cannot take you. We already have our exact number,' replied Maeldun, his voice rising above the wind.

'Turn back, or we will swim after you till we are drowned,' shouted the brothers, plunging in and striking out towards the vessel.

When Maeldun saw that they meant to do this, he felt he had no choice but to take them on board, so he turned back and watched as strong arms helped the swimmers over the pitching stern of the curragh and onto the deck.

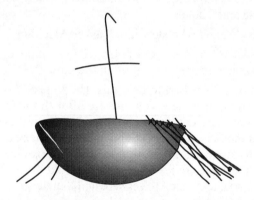

Model curragh (National Museum of Ireland, Dublin)

They rowed that day and night and all the next day and evening. At midnight they glimpsed by moonlight two small islands with large dwellings on them. It was a still night and when they raised the oars and drifted close, they could hear merriment and conversation on the island. Then they heard two men arguing drunkenly, one of them saying: 'I'm a better warrior than you, for I slew Allil Ocar Aga and burned the church over his head, and no one dares to seek revenge against me. You have never done a deed to equal that!'

Hearing this, Maeldun's friends Germane and Diuran rejoiced that they had been guided here so quickly and urged Maeldun to sack the place immediately and avenge his father's death. But even as they spoke a wind blew up and clouds blotted out the moon and in moments a great storm was driving them away. It kept up all that night and well into the next day and when it grew calm they found they were far off in unknown seas.

'Take down the sail and put up the oars and let us drift in whatever direction God pleases,' ordered Maeldun. Turning to his three foster-brothers he added, 'This evil has come to us because we broke from the prescription of the druid Nuca and took you on board when we already had our full complement of men.'

The brothers shifted uneasily at this, but remained silent.

The curragh sailed on for three days and nights, until they came to an island where they sighted flocks of hungry-looking ants the size of foals milling down to the beach as if intent on eating both men and craft. But this was only the first of many strange islands. They came next to an isle of many-coloured birds and then one inhabited by a monstrous blue-clawed animal, another where a demon horse-race was taking place and yet another where they were mysteriously fed without any trace of their benefactor. From the next island Maeldun procured a wondrous cluster of seven apples, each of which supplied the adventurers with food and drink for forty days and forty nights.

There followed an island of animals that ate each other. Then came one inhabited by an extraordinary monster who first revolved his bones and flesh inside his skin, then revolved his skin around his bones and flesh, and finally revolved his upper skin and lower skin in opposite directions. When he saw the curragh turning back he hurled stones at them with surprising accuracy, and they were lucky to escape.

After this came an isle of red-hot animals like pigs that fed on golden apples all day, leaving them to flocks of birds at night. Here the men were able to procure quantities of the apples by night to sustain them for many days.

After rowing for days and finishing their supply of apples, they came to a little island on which was a large palace. The men rowed close and dropped anchor and then went ashore to see who or what they would find. The snow-white palace was surrounded by a pure-white wall. Inside they found no feasting warriors, although there was a feast laid out. To their surprise the one living creature there was a little cat, which occupied the main chamber. This creature looked up at Maeldun and his crew for a moment and then continued its play, which consisted of leaping to and from the tops of a number of low, square marble pillars standing in a row.

Investigating their surroundings the men found first a quantity of precious brooches of gold and silver, with torcs and great swords of the same gleaming metals. Around the room were arranged pure-white couches, excellent cooked meats and strong ale.

'Is this food for us?' asked Maeldun of the little cat, which looked up for a moment and then continued its play. Concluding that the food was indeed intended for them, Maeldun invited his men to eat and drink their fill. They did so and then slept soundly on the fine couches.

When they awoke, Maeldun's eldest foster-brother asked him, 'Shall I bring one of those large torcs away?'

'Certainly not,' replied Maeldun without hesitation. 'We're lucky to have been fed and rested. Touch nothing, for the house must be under someone's guard.'

Ignoring this advice the foster-brother took down a great gold torc and set off for the shore. But the cat bounded after him and, springing at him like an arrow of fire, shot straight through the unfortunate young man's body, reducing it to ashes. Then the cat returned quietly to the chamber and resumed its play upon the marble pillars.

Maeldun picked up the torc, spoke softly to the cat and returned the prize to its former place. Then he gathered up his foster-brother's ashes, spread them on the sea and ordered the men to set sail.

After this, Maeldun's party came to an island where a man was dividing white and black sheep. When he took a white sheep and flung it over a wall to join the black ones, it became black. When he flung a black sheep in with the white ones, it became white. Maeldun flung a black stick ashore into the white section to see what would happen, and sure enough it became white. The crew had no wish to be turned either black or white and so they sailed away.

The next island featured a burning river and huge calves guarded by an equally huge cowherd. Then came an island where a burly miller flung huge quantities of corn, cattle and wealth of every description into his mill. He explained that this was the Mill of Invertre-Kenand and in it was ground anything with which men were in any way dissatisfied or which they tried to conceal from God.

Shortly after this they came to the Isle of Weeping. All its inhabitants wept continuously or wrung their hands and sighed. It fell to the lot of Maeldun's second foster-brother to explore this island. He went among the people and soon became equally sorrowful. Two of the crew went to fetch him back, but were unable to find him among the tearful throng. Worse, they too became deeply miserable and could only be fetched back by four men whom Maeldun instructed to cover their mouths and noses and to look only at each other while on the island. The four men were saved, but the second foster-brother had to be left behind.

There followed an island divided into four by walls of gold, silver, copper and crystal and then one with a palace reached only by a crystal bridge which flung them back every time they attempted to cross it. In both these islands they were given a food that looked like cheese, but which tasted to each man exactly like his favourite food. In the second, tinkling bells sent the men into a peaceful sleep.

Sailing on they came to an island of talking birds, one inhabited by a hermit fed by angels and one of giant blacksmiths who pelted them with hot iron. Then they sailed across a crystal sea and saw a beautiful land beneath the waves – only to discover that its inhabitants were plagued by a flesh-eating monster. There was an island where women pelted them with nuts, and another where salmon fell out of a miraculous rainbow water-arch.

The next wonder was hardly an island at all, but an immense eight-sided silver pillar jutting straight out of the iron-grey sea. From its top hung a silver net whose mesh was so large that the curragh was able to sail through it. Diuran took his spear and broke off a bit of the mesh. Maeldun warned him not to destroy it, but Diuran said, 'I did it for the glory of God and so that our story will be more readily believed. If we ever return, I'll lay this silver as an offering on the altar at Armagh Cathedral.'

After passing another island consisting of a single pillar with a locked door, they reached a fair-sized island where an impressive palace was clearly visible from some distance out at sea. Rowing closer the men saw that the palace was richly decorated, a joy to behold. They landed and soon saw a number of lovely maidens. They sat and rested and after a while they saw a rider approaching: a young woman richly dressed in a blue silk headdress and a purple cloak. One of the maidens held her horse while she dismounted. She entered the palace and presently Maeldun and his men were invited in to meet the woman – who was in fact the queen of the island. She welcomed them in and saw to it that they were well fed and that Maeldun drank from a crystal goblet.

The next day the Queen spoke to Maeldun and his men: 'There is no need for you to go wandering over the wide ocean. Remain in my country. Here you will never grow old and die and you will live a life of pleasure and ease.'

A few of the men looked as if they found this a tempting prospect, but especially Maeldun himself, who was already half in love with the queen. She told them she was widowed and that every day she went to administer justice among her people – but that Maeldun and his crew should stay in the palace and take their ease.

The men spent the three winter months on the island, although by the end it seemed to them as if three years had passed, for they longed for their homeland – all except Maeldun, who argued that they would find nothing at home that they did not already have on the island.

'Maeldun loves the Queen of the island,' they said to each other. 'Let him stay here while we return home.'

Maeldun, however, would not remain without his companions and so they planned to leave. Now one day when the Queen had gone to deliver justice to her people, the men prepared their curragh and put out to sea. The wading birds had not yet settled again on the beach before the Queen appeared. She saw what was happening and quickly fetched a large ball of thread. She then stood on the shore and flung the ball, keeping a tight grip on one end. She aimed well, and Maeldun standing in the stern of the *curragh* caught the ball and it stuck fast to his hand. The Queen then pulled gently on the thread and easily drew the vessel back to land.

Thus the travellers stayed another nine months on the island – and all against their will except for Maeldun. Several times they tried to leave, but each time the Queen returned with the ball of thread and it was caught by Maeldun so that they were all pulled back to the island. The men therefore agreed that, next time, another man should catch the ball. The next time came and the man chosen caught the ball, but it clung as determinedly to his hand as it had to Maeldun's. The Queen began to wind them in, but Diuran drew his sword and sliced off the man's hand, so that they were able to escape – leaving behind them the Queen and her maidens lamenting on the shore.

After this the voyagers landed on an island of intoxicating fruits, and then on one inhabited by a holy man, the sole survivor of fifteen pilgrims. While here they saw a strange sight. A huge bird landed on a hill and began to eat fruit from a branch. Then two others appeared and carefully preened the bird, which was evidently very old. On the third day the younger pair flew off and the old bird bathed in a little lake, emerging with all his youth restored. Maeldun's friend Diuran resolved to try the same. The other men had doubts, but Diuran plunged into the lake and from that day he never got any older.

They came then to the Land of Laughter and here Maeldun's third foster-brother drew the lot to explore the island. He became caught up in the infectious laughter of those on the island, and though the crew waited for him, he never returned.

Next, as they sailed across the waves they became aware of something bright in the distance, and as they approached they saw it was an island surrounded by a revolving rampart of fire. There was a single door in the rampart and whenever it faced the sea the men could catch a glimpse of festivities going on within. But rather than landing they ventured on.

Soon after this they came to a bare rock with another hermit standing on it. He was so old that his body was entirely covered in white hair. He told them that he had been a wicked, pilfering cook to a monastery, but that an old man sitting on the waves had made him see the error of his ways. He had begun to repent, and was sustained by seven cakes and a cup of whey given to him by the old man, and then by salmon brought to him by otters. The hermit, now grown so old, assured Maeldun and his crew that they would reach their homes and that on the way Maeldun would find the man who killed his father. At this, Maeldun started up.

'But', added the old hermit, 'you must not kill him or in any way take revenge. As God has protected and forgiven you, so must you forgive this man.'

Soon they saw an island over which hovered a falcon that they recognized as one of the falcons of Ireland. By this they knew they had not far to go. First, however, they had to encounter the murderer of Allil, Maeldun's father.

Finding themselves at last approaching the islands they had come to at the start of their long wanderings, before the storm had swept them away, they went ashore and stode towards the great house there, with Maeldun at their head. Reaching the house, they overheard another conversation.

'It would not be well for you if Maeldun were here.'

'Maeldun!' replied the other. 'It is well known that he died long ago at sea.'

'Don't be so sure. Perhaps he is the very man who will wake you from sleep one morning!'

Another voice asked, 'What would you do if he were to arrive?'

Allil's murderer responded wholeheartedly: 'That's easy to answer. If Maeldun is indeed alive, then he has for a long time been suffering great hardships. If he were to come now, though we were once enemies, I would welcome him with all my heart.'

Hearing this, Maeldun knocked at the door and was invited in. 'I am Maeldun, returned safe from my wanderings.'

The man who had promised to welcome Maeldun was as good as his word, inviting him and his men to stay and feast till they forgot their hardships and weary years upon the waves. Neither was there any talk of past misdeeds. Maeldun and his crew told the story of their adventures and after some days returned home. And Diuran, good to his word, took the silver he had struck from the silver net at sea and laid it on the high altar at Armagh Cathedral.

COMMENTARY

This tale is in a genre known as *immrama*, sea voyage quests, and in many ways it resembles the *Odyssey* or Jason's quest for the Golden Fleece. It begins as a quest for revenge but turns into a voyage of self-discovery. Through failing to adhere to the druid's prescription as to the number of men who should accompany him, Maeldun brings on himself – and his men – a long voyage full of dangers and hardships, as well as wonders. It is as if paganism, in the shape of the druid, rules at the start of the story, with Maeldun being punished for offending the old powers instead of being rewarded for taking pity on his foster-brothers, while Christianity takes over at the end.

The pagan context and the Christian moral

Although the moral of the story is a Christian one – 'Forgive those who trespass against you' – the context of what precedes this is pagan. First, we have Maeldun as the semi-orphan who has to go in search of his true parentage. Then, once he has found out the truth about his father, he has to avenge him. This is a variation on myths, both in Celtic and other cultures, in which a son has to find his father, often undergoing heroic tests on the way. Examples include the Greek stories of Theseus and Oedipus, and the Pawnee tale of the Medicine Grizzly Bear. Cuchulainn has to go in search of a foster-father (see page 16); and when his own son comes in search of him, Cuchulainn kills him without realizing his identity (as nearly happens to Theseus): the search for the male principle is an initiation fraught with danger. The variation for Maeldun is that he has to find his own manhood by avenging his father and thus prove himself worthy of him.

Another aspect of the mythological hero's quest, and sometimes of the father search, is that the young hero is sent off by a negative male figure. In Native American myths this is often an uncle (who might also be a foster-father). For the Greek hero Jason it is Pelias, while for Perseus it is his mother's suitor. The 'sender' usually hopes that the young man will die in the attempt. In the case of Maeldun we have only the shadowy figure of Bricka, but he conforms to type in that he is unpleasant and goads the hero into action. He may be connected to Bricriu, the 'poison-tongued' mischief maker who in the *Tain Bo Cuailnge* taunts Cuchulainn when he is down, probably saving his life by doing so, and even to the Norse god Loki.

On another level Maeldun's voyage is a passage through the Otherworld (see pages 4–5). It may be that the story was intended to provide the soul with a map of the afterlife, something like both the Egyptian and Tibetan Books of the Dead. Certainly many details of the voyage suggest the Otherworld, such as wondrous apples, food that takes on the taste of whatever each man most wants, beautiful women who are almost impossible to leave, and a city beneath the waves.

Setting sail

The Celts, in common with most ancient cultures, believed that each moment in time, or at least each day, had a particular quality making it suitable for specific enterprises. We have seen this in the case of Cuchulainn, whose taking up of arms on a particular day determines his short but glorious life. Maeldun carefully observes the druid's recommendations for starting to build his craft and for setting sail. One could speculate about the significance of the number 60 as the number of crew that Maeldun is told to take with him. For example, it is double the number of islands that he subsequently visits. However, no particular meaning stands out.

What is more clear is that when the three foster-brothers make their threat he is faced with a dilemma: he has to choose between obedience to druidry and Christian charity. In a sense, too, he has to take the brothers with him because they are aspects of himself and of his old life. He is not yet ready to leave these behind.

The islands

Many of the islands Maeldun visits are threatening in some way: the giant ants, the demons, the strange monster revolving inside his skin, rather like Cuchulainn going into his 'Warp-Spasm' (see page 16). Others are mysteriously sustaining, like the one where an invisible benefactor provides a feast, or the land of the red-hot animals where the men find apples on which they live for days. This sustenance, especially in the form of apples, or food that takes on whatever taste each man wants, suggests the infant fantasy of the perpetually available, all-sustaining breast – or, in other terms, the goddess. Other islands suggest illusions taken as real in the temporal world, which must be discarded in the spiritual world.

The first island described in any detail is the one where the little cat provides an unlikely but effective threshold guardian. Maeldun seems to understand the animal, and although he does not foresee exactly what happens, he knows well enough that the first foster-brother should not repay hospitality with theft. The brother is dramatically reduced to ashes by his own greedy materialism. It should also be noted that in some Celtic myths, as in 'Diarmuid and Grainne', the cat is a symbol of death.

The island that follows, where the man is dividing black and white sheep, suggests the dynamic relationship between opposites: night and day, male and female, yin and yang, good and evil. The fact that the sheep change colour according to which side of the wall they are suggests that these opposites are in a sense illusory: to an enlightened mind they are the same as each other or are at least just the same energy taking different forms.

The mill that grinds everything with which men have been dissatisfied, or which they have tried to hide from God, is obviously coloured by Christian belief. At the same time, it could contain the germ of something older: the idea that one should accept one's lot or that the 'bread of sorrow' is made from a negative outlook. A more extreme negativity reigns on the next island, where the second foster-brother succumbs to its mood of despair and is lost to Maeldun. Symbolically, Maeldun is putting aside despondency in favour of hope.

The next island, with its four walls of gold, silver, copper and crystal may refer to the four ages of the world or to the illusory nature of divisions. The food the men receive on this island is like ambrosia and is clearly Otherworldly in that it is exactly what each man wants – again hinting at mother's milk. On the next island, the crystal bridge which flings the men back when they try to cross it is a familiar motif. In other stories, as in that of Cuchulainn going to train with the warrior druidess Scathach, the bridge provides a test for the hero, who finds a way to cross it. Rather frustratingly for us, this fails to happen in Maeldun's story and the outcome of their visit to this island is inconclusive. However, both the tinkling music that sends them into a gentle sleep, and the wonderful food that has similar qualities to that which they receive on the previous island, are very Otherworldly.

The talking birds and giant blacksmiths who pelt the men with hot iron represent further wonders and dangers, while the crystal sea and the beautiful land beneath the waves seem to suggest both the riches and dangers of the unconscious and of the spirit world. The nuts with which they are pelted and salmon falling out of the rainbow water-arch, both suggest the acquisition of wisdom (see Finn and the Salmon of Wisdom, pages 33–39). The silver net through whose mesh the curragh sails represents a test that the men pass, as if successfully crossing a threshold. We see Maeldun's wisdom in his telling Diuran not to destroy the mesh and more Christian overlay in Diuran's insistence on taking back a bit of the net 'for the glory of God' and to give their story credibility.

The episode of the island on which Maeldun is apparently much taken by the beautiful queen is full of potent symbolism which can be interpreted on a number of levels. A Freudian might point out that the queen is widowed – like Maeldun's own mother. Maeldun could fulfil the Oedipal infantile fantasy by forgetting about his quest for revenge and marrying the queen. There is no need for him to kill the husband and father figure: he has already been disposed of! Maeldun is certainly in danger of losing his motivation, as we see by his argument for staying put rather than sailing for home.

When they do finally try to sail away, only to be tugged back in by the sticky ball of thread, Maeldun's attachment to the queen is to blame. There are echoes of Ariadne's thread here: Theseus finds his way back out of the womb-like labyrinth by means of the thread. The thread is like an umbilical cord and, in the case of Maeldun, what happens strongly evokes reincarnation, by which the soul is tugged back to the womb and the world by its material attachments. Note, especially, that after this first return the men are obliged to remain another nine months before they try to escape again. Drastic action has to be taken to avoid this happening for ever and so Maeldun's friend Diuran, in the familiar mythic role of 'helper' to the hero, slices off the hand of the unfortunate man. This man is a replacement for Maeldun, but also an aspect of him: Maeldun has to make a sacrifice in order to progress. Diuran's sword is clearly a male symbol, but it is also the sword of wisdom and discernment, like the sword of the bodhisattva Manjushri in Buddhist mythology.

The rejuvenating bird on the next island represents reincarnation and spiritual rebirth. Diuran is rewarded for his courage by the gift of unfading youthfulness. Birds themselves symbolize the spirit in its ability to soar above the material world.

Maeldun's third and last foster-brother is lost on the Island of Laughter. Whereas the previous brother was lost to despair, this one succumbs to frivolity. So, in the three brothers, as aspects of Maeldun, we see the questing hero's putting aside of material greed, despair and frivolity. With these obstacles to spiritual progress overcome, Maeldun is now almost ready to receive the wisdom that the story presents as the main reward for his hardships. First, he must glimpse a land of feasting through a revolving wall of fire, suggesting the Celtic circle of death and rebirth, with the recurring opportunities for incarnation – with, of course, more than a hint of Christian hellfire! Next, he encounters the penitent hermit, who has fed on the Salmon of Wisdom and advises Maeldun not to seek revenge. Maeldun evidently takes this advice to heart.

The ending of the story is very odd, not so much in that Maeldun chooses Christian forgiveness rather than revenge, but in that so little is made of the fact. One might expect Maeldun to confront his father's murderer, and then to say, 'But I forgive you.' Instead, although Maeldun overhears the crime alluded to by the man and his companions, Maeldun himself does not even mention it. Perhaps by saying he would welcome Maeldun if he ever walked in, the murderer almost literally 'takes the wind out of his sails'.

The tale has a nicely rounded Christian ending in Diuran's keeping his promise to put the silver he took from the mesh on the altar of Armagh Cathedral (St Patrick's, built in 445). However, one wonders if the original oral version of the story had Maeldun fighting a terrible battle with the murdering plunderer, slaying him, then triumphantly taking over his birthright as his father's son: namely, the leadership of his tribe. His name does, after all, mean 'Chief of the Fort'. The ending we have instead would probably have seemed very puzzling to pre-fifth-century Celts raised on the far bloodthirstier tales of Cuchulainn and similar heroes.

12 | PWLL AND ARAWN

The story of Pwll's meeting with Arawn, Lord of Annwn (in Welsh myths the Underworld or Otherworld), makes up the first part of the first 'branch' of the *Mabinogion*. The remainder of the branch recounts how Pwll meets and marries the Otherworld woman Rhiannon.

One day Pwll, Lord of Dyfed, felt drawn to the hunt. So he gave orders for preparations to be made and early the next morning he set out from his court at Arberth accompanied by his nobles and servants. They made a fine sight as they passed out of the fortress, the horses fresh, the hounds straining at the leash and already searching for a scent on the autumn air. Women waved to their men as they went, children to their fathers. No woman, however, waved to Pwll, as at that time he had no wife.

Pwll had decided to hunt in a secluded glen two days' journey away. That night the party camped out, and the following morning they rose early and set off. The sun struck the dew raised by the dogs' paws as they raced eagerly into the woods. Pwll blew his horn and followed after the dogs, enjoying his horse's strength and speed and his own mastery of the animal. Soon he realized that he had left the rest of his party behind. Still he followed the baying and yelping of his hounds as they sped through the forest. Then, as the trees seemed to come closer together and he found himself having to weave between their trunks and duck beneath their branches, he heard the sound of another pack of dogs whose hunting cry approached from far off, echoing, yet distinct from, that of his own pack.

Presently Pwll's horse burst into a large clearing of level ground. At the same moment a stag burst panting out of the trees on the far side of the clearing, closely pursued by the strange pack. As Pwll drew close, he hardly noticed the stag, because his attention was taken by the appearance of the hounds: dazzling white, except for their ears, which shone red as setting suns. Even so, he gave scarcely a thought as he drove them away from the falling stag and baited his own hounds upon it. As he did this another figure appeared swiftly from between the trees, an imposing huntsman dressed in grey-brown and mounted on a big dapple-grey horse. He looked angry.

'Chieftain,' thundered the stranger, 'I know who you are, but I do not greet you.'

'Well,' answered Pwll, 'perhaps that is because your high rank prevents it.'

'It is not my rank but your discourtesy in driving off my hounds, which ran down this stag and setting on your own pack in their place.'

Pwll shifted in the saddle. 'Chieftain,' he began, conciliatingly, 'if I have wronged you I will earn your friendship in a way befitting your rank. Just tell me who you are.'

'I am Arawn, King of Annwn and you can earn my friendship by changing places with me for a year. I will rule your kingdom and you will go into Annwn and rule there in my place. I will cloak you in my own appearance so that even my wife will be deceived and you will be obeyed by all.'

'I see,' said Pwll. 'And is there anything else?'

'Yes. I have an enemy, Havgan of Arawn. He rules the kingdom bordering mine and he continually wages war against me. A year from tonight I am to meet him in single combat at the ford on the river separating our two kingdoms. Take my place and rid me of him and you will earn my everlasting friendship. But be warned: strike only one blow. He will not survive it. Don't try to finish him off, even if he begs you.'

Pwll gladly agreed and Arawn led him deeper into the woods and out into the open air, where at last they could see the outlying defences of Arawn's kingdom. Arawn rode off and was soon swallowed up by the forest. Pwll trotted on and came within sight of a fine palace. Soon he was hailed respectfully by servants who led his horse to the stables, ran ahead of him to his quarters and then helped him out of his hunting clothes and into a suit of gold brocade. Before long he was seated at the head of the table in the great hall, with the Queen, who was even more beautiful than he had imagined, sitting beside him.

The evening passed in sumptuous feasting and merriment and Pwll thought his queenly companion the most gracious woman he had ever met. However, when bedtime came and the pair retired together to the royal chamber, Pwll forced himself to behave as he felt he should out of loyalty to Arawn. He tore his eyes away from the beautiful young queen beside him, quietly turned his back on her and went to sleep. The next day he was once again tender and affectionate towards her, but each night he made himself behave in the same way.

Over the next year the days passed pleasantly enough for Pwll, although every night he had to exercise all his self-control in bed with the queen. At last the appointed day came when Pwll was to meet Havgan in single combat at the ford. It was another bright autumn day and he rode out to the borders of the kingdom as if once again to the hunt. Nobles accompanied him, but at the river they hung back. All knew that the combat was to be solely between the two kings. Havgan was waiting on the other side of the broad but shallow river, his nobles also keeping a respectful distance. On each side the horses' hooves clattered on the glistening, round stones, then splashed in the water as they paced towards the centre. Mid-stream the two men spurred their horses into a charge and on this first rush Pwll struck such a mighty blow that Havgan's shield and armour split and Havgan was thrown, mortally wounded, into the river.

With difficulty, the fallen man spoke. 'I don't know what you had against me, but since you have defeated me, I pray you, put me out of my misery.'

'Anyone who wishes may strike you again,' answered Pwll, 'but I will not.'

With that, the stricken Havgan surrendered hope and he called on his followers to carry him away to die. Thus Arawn, through Pwll, became king of both kingdoms.

Pwll now rode away alone towards the place where he had agreed to meet Arawn. The real King of Annwn was there in the glen waiting for him and both men were delighted to see each other again, Arawn all the more so for being rid of his old enemy Havgan.

Arawn restored Pwll's own appearance and rode to his own court. He was pleased to see it after the long year's absence, although his arrival was treated with no special ceremony by his countrymen, who of course had been unaware of his absence. Arawn spent his day pleasurably and at night-time he accompanied his queen to their bed chamber. Alone with her at last he at once began to caress her. She was amazed, and commented that this was the first time in a year that he had so much as turned his face to hers in bed. Arawn then explained the situation to his queen and both marvelled at the strength of character shown by Pwll in keeping faith with his friend and resisting temptation.

Back in Dyfed, Pwll was enjoying his homecoming. Being somewhat circumspect, he asked his nobles, 'Tell me, how well have I ruled you and the kingdom over the last year?' Each replied that he had been even more wise, kind and generous than ever. 'Then you should thank the man who ruled here in my place,' he confessed, promising them to continue to rule in the same fashion.

After this, Pwll and Arawn became firm friends, sending each other bright-eyed falcons, thoroughbred horses and swift hounds, as well as other treasures. And since Pwll had ruled so well in Annwn and had united the kingdoms by his courage and skill, the name 'Lord of Dyfed' fell out of use. Instead, he came to be called Pwll, Head of Annwn.

COMMENTARY

In this story the hero goes on what may originally have been a shamanistic journey to the Otherworld (see page 4). He is hunting, which is a form of quest, and on one level what he seeks is his real self. He cannot find himself when he is surrounded by the distractions and responsibilities of normal life, but a magical transformation begins to occur when he is separated from the rest of his party and goes deeper into the uncharted regions of the forest, which is also the realm of the unconscious.

It is often the case in myth that a hero is led into the spiritual world, or the world of the unconscious, by a magical beast. In an Arapaho story a girl pursues a porcupine up an ever-extending tree and finds herself in the spirit world; in the Greek tale Achtaeon is led to his fatal encounter with the goddess Artemis by the deer which he is hunting. For Pwll, that beast is the stag, but the two sets of hounds are also significant. Pwll hears the strange hounds off in the distance, echoing the baying of his own pack, as the two realities approach each other. At the key moment of illumination – made physically possible by the clearing in the forest – Pwll makes an error. He ungraciously sets his own hounds on another man's stag. Moreover, he does this despite the strange pack having the colouring that in other Celtic myths, such as Oisin's journey to the Otherworld (see page 88), identifies them as Otherworldly. Having committed this error, he must atone for it.

Pwll's atonement – at-one-ment – can only come about by his entirely taking on the role of the ruler of the Otherworld. In fact their exchange of roles and appearances is so complete that we have to regard them as being aspects of one person, especially since Pwll eventually comes to be known as Pwll, Head of Annwn. Most peculiar is the fact that even Arawn's wife is not told, and never suspects, that she is now sharing her bed with a different man. Pwll's self-restraint in respect of the queen is the first way in which he atones for his earlier transgression. It also makes him worthy of his own Otherworldly queen Rhiannon, whom he meets in a later part of his story.

However, his restraint is also remarkable in being so unlike earlier Celtic tales, in which no special virtue is ascribed to sexual abstinence. True, in the *Tain Bo Cuailnge* Fergus feels guilty about having slept with Queen Medb, wife of Ailill, but it is no great crime. In fact Medb herself on several occasions offers to any man who can slay Cuchulainn a package of rewards which includes her 'friendly thighs' as part of the bargain. Cuchulainn himself almost never turns down an offer of sex. There is even a story, which may be directly linked to that of Pwll, in which Cuchulainn, as a result of falling into a possibly shamanistic trance, goes to the Otherworld and lives with the fairy wife of the god Manannan mac Lir. He earns her by fighting for just one day against her brother's enemy, which echoes Pwll's agreement to fight Havgan.

The restraint shown by Pwll would seem to come from the influence of French chivalric tales, which would have found their way more easily into Dyfed, from which the story originates, than into the mountain fastnesses of Gwynnedd. The chivalric tales were in turn influenced by Christian morality. Another tale which must be linked to that of Pwll is the Arthurian story of Gawain and the Green Knight, in which Gawain has to exercise similar self-restraint in relation to the Green Knight's wife.

The test which Pwll passes is less explicit: Arawn's wife makes no advances towards him and on the face of it he would actually be justified in treating her fully as his own wife. Then, just as Gawain has to undertake a test of courage, Pwll has to go (also a year later) to meet Arawn's enemy Havgan. They meet at the border between the kingdoms, fighting at a ford – which appears elsewhere in Celtic myth as a place of single combat (in the *Tain Bo Cuailnge* Cuchulainn fights his single combats at a ford). This location could be seen as a meeting point between two levels of consciousness or between the spiritual Otherworld and the material world. Alternatively it could relate to a ritual combat between the seasons. Jeffrey Gatz tentatively identifies the sombrely dressed Arawn with winter and says that Havgan may mean 'summer white'. The Green Knight seems to represent the life-force that survives winter. But in Celtic myth there is no clear distinction between the Otherworld and the Underworld and the Otherworld is also called the 'Summer Land'. In addition, Annwn can as easily be translated as 'Not-World'.

Beyond the seasonal interpretation, by passing his tests and making atonement Pwll achieves a union between this world and the Otherworld or between the material world and the spiritual. In a shamanistic sense he does this on behalf of his people, resolving a communal conflict by his inner journey, which is presented in the myth as an external one.

13 | THE DROWNED CITY OF YS

This well-known Breton legend was collected in the *Barzaz Breiz*, or Songs of Brittany. The island-city of Ys is thought by some to have been located off the west coast of Brittany, beyond the Pointe du Raz in the Baie des Trepasses, otherwise known as the Bay of the Dead. Others locate it off the end of the causeway of Penmarc'h.

There was once a king named Gradlon who ruled over the kingdom of Cornouaille. He had a daughter, Dahut-Ahes, whose dark hair, pale face and black eyes resembled those of her vanished mother. Her mother had been half human. She had come from the sea and cast an enchantment on Gradlon, who became infatuated with her. But, despite her warnings, one day he displeased her, so she left him, disappearing back under the waves.

For many years Gradlon and Dahut lived in harmony together. He loved her beauty and her wildness and if she asked for anything, he would give it to her. Then one day Gradlon went out hunting in the great forest of Menez-Hom and pursued a wild boar for so long that he and his men became exhausted and gave up the chase. Finding themselves near an old hut, they asked for hospitality. The hut was inhabited by a hermit who welcomed them and offered to give them a meal. He took a fish, sliced it in half and threw half back into a well where it immediately became whole again. He then began to cook the other half, which – to the men's astonishment – miraculously turned into a sumptuous banquet. Impressed by this, Gradlon asked the hermit Corentin to return with him to his palace at Quimper. After much persuasion, Corentin finally agreed to go with him. Not long afterwards Gradlon converted to Christianity and appointed Corentin Bishop of Cornouaille. Together they set about building numerous churches and chapels all over the land.

But as the Christianizing of the land increased, Dahut began to sicken and become listless. Often she would gaze out to sea, weeping and sighing. When Gradlon asked her what the matter was she told him she was suffering because the land was now full of prayer and penitence and there was no longer any joy or laughter anywhere. She longed for the sea, she said, and would only feel better if he would build a city for her beside the water where she could live in harmony with the elements.

So, to please his daughter, Gradlon built the fabled city of Ys, sometimes known as Ker-Ys, 'the beloved place'. It lay on a spit of land that jutted out into the sea. Graced with towers, fine houses, fountains, courtyards, wide avenues and cobbled streets, it was so splendid that Gradlon decided to move there himself and live with his daughter, leaving Corentin to administer Quimper. But when Corentin came to visit him he noticed that among all the beautiful new buildings there was not a single church in the whole of Ys. Gradlon immediately promised to rectify the situation but Dahut argued that it was far more urgent that the city should be protected from the danger of flooding. After this she decided it was time to visit the mysterious Isle of Sein, so one night she secretly left the palace and set out alone in a small boat.

It was a dangerous journey, for no one who feared for their lives would venture anywhere near the island. It was inhabited by a sisterhood of druidesses who received and tended the souls of the dead. Moreover, these nine priestesses of the old magic, the last of their kind in Brittany, still retained the ability to shape-shift and were served by the Korrigans, an ancient race of dwarfish elemental beings.

As Dahut approached the island she was enveloped by the mist that hung heavily round its shores and threatened by the huge waves beating on its rocks, but she stood up defiantly in her coracle, plucking the strings of a bardic harp and calling on her lost mother's powers. She beached safely and, drawing her wet clothes around her, wandered inland. She saw a path etched in moonlight on the fringes of a forest and followed it, coming at last to a grove deep in the woodland. There she found the dark-robed sisters, tending a burning brazier. She came up to them boldly and announced herself, asking for help for her city which was being threatened by the new faith. The druidesses agreed to help her and commanded the Korrigans to construct a great dyke around the city to protect it from flooding. They also commanded them to build a lavish castle that would tower over the new church.

All this was accomplished and soon an impressive castle appeared straddling the torrent of Huelgoat, and at the same time a thick stone wall arose round the city, held by a huge bronze sluice gate. Dahut entrusted its golden key to her father, who wore it round his neck, and the fame of the city went far and wide, as did the fame of the strange and lovely Dahut herself.

Because of this, many young men were lured to Ys. Dahut always received them, inviting them to feast in her great palace and, if any of them pleased her, she would leave orders for him to be conducted to her chamber. First, he would be masked, then led down narrow corridors to her bedroom by her black-robed servant. But when she had tired of him, the mask swiftly became an instrument of death, crushing his skull, after which his body would be thrown into the torrent beneath the castle to join the other drowned lovers, trapped forever in the wave-sucked caves of Huelgoat.

Gradlon, meanwhile, was so spellbound by his daughter that he turned a blind eye to her cruelty. Ys rose in fame and riches until gradually the whole city became corrupted by soft living. Feasting and carousing was the order of the day, while the neglected church fell into disrepair. When news of this state of affairs reached Corentin he went to Guénolé, Abbot of Landévennec, and asked him to intervene. Guénolé journeyed toYs and was appalled by the godlessness of the city. He began preaching the gospel in the streets but was treated with contempt.

Soon after this a new suitor arrived at Dahut's castle. Dressed in crimson silk beneath a finely embroidered red velvet cloak, he was so imperious and compelling that Dahut was irresistibly drawn to him. When she invited him to her chamber he refused to wear the proferred mask, and when he reached her room he refused to make love to her until she promised to grant his request. Then he asked for the key to the sluice-gate in the dyke. Dahut was so infatuated that she stole into her father's chamber where he lay sleeping, took the golden key from his neck and handed it to her lover.

Without a second glance at her, the tall red-cloaked figure strode out to the great sluice-gate, fitted the key in the lock and turned it. Immediately the dark water began to surge into the city. Gradlon woke at the cries of his daughter and ran to the stables, where he mounted his horse and, with Dahut clinging on behind him, raced for land, the waters rising behind them. But spur as he might, his horse seemed to be held back by a deadly weight. Guénolé, appearing at that moment, shouted above the uproar, telling the King to cast from his horse the demon that was hindering him. Gradlon refused to believe he had other than his daughter with him, so Guénolé reached out with his staff and struck Dahut, pushing her off the horse and into the waves. Immediately the sea became calm and Gradlon was able to reach land safely, but behind him the streets and houses, towers and turrets were already engulfed as Ys sank slowly beneath the waves.

And there it lies still, drowned and silent. Except that, on wild nights, Breton fishermen have sometimes reported hearing the clashing of a bell from deep under water or strange sighing and singing which rises momentarily from the swirling depths before dying away again. Some also swear they have seen Dahut herself, a flash of wild hair, dark eyes in a white face, a pale thin-fingered hand above the waves.

> *J'ai vu la blanche fille de la mer,*
> *je l'ai même entendue chanter.*

(Barzaz Breiz)

COMMENTARY

Like most Breton legends, this is set in the fifth century CE, when paganism was giving way to Christianity. Gradlon was known as Gradlon-Meur, or Gradlon the Great. Ys is believed to have existed and to have been the capital of Cornouaille. Gradlon was converted after visiting Guénolé and subsequently gave Cornouaille its first bishop, Corentin. After the sinking of Ys, which is believed still to be below the sea, Gradlon went to live in Quimper, where a statue of him on horseback can be seen between the spires of the Cathedral. The *Barzaz Breiz* records an annual custom that used to be carried out on St Cecilia's Day, in which a minstrel would climb up and offer the statue a drink of wine, after which he would throw the goblet down to the crowd below. This ritual ended with the French Revolution.

Another tradition says that after the death of Dahut, Gradlon retreated to the forest of Kranou where he lived with a druid. When Guénolé found him there he was dying. The king asked the Abbot not to deal harshly with the old druid who was mourning a dead religion.

Mermaids and water deities

Tales of mermaids form a strong part of Breton culture. Dahut was renamed Ahes or Mary Morgan and became known as the Mermaid of Brittany. Her mother also appears to have been a mermaid figure. The image of the mermaid or water goddess is therefore a very important one in the story.

Celtic figure with serpent legs and fishtail feet (carved stone in National Museum of Scotland)

The water goddess was an ancient deity, dwelling in the waters of life and linked with the tides to the moon. She had life-giving qualities and was a type of Great Mother. The Irish water deity Liban could shape-shift into the Salmon of Wisdom (see pages 33–39). Thus there is a link between the fishtail of the mermaid and intuitive wisdom. The fish also symbolizes regeneration (see page 36). The famous French mermaid Melusina is depicted as having a serpent's tail rather than that of a fish. However, the serpent has been equally regarded as a symbol of wisdom – also of regeneration because of its ability to shed its skin. In fact, all half-human, half-animal women, such as the silkies (seal-women) and the Sirens (bird-women), were originally seen as possessing attributes of an ancient, intuitive wisdom that constituted an important part of their divinity.

But as the new religion of Christianity grew in strength, so the old one declined. The half-human and half-animal women came to be regarded not as divine guardians of a deep wisdom, but as sub-human. The scaly fishtail of the mermaid became more allied with that of the serpent, which itself was now particularly feared. Its original association with regeneration and the life-force was narrowed until it became associated exclusively with sexuality. Sexuality itself, which had at one time been venerated, was now seen as something sinful that had to be suppressed. Alongside this came a reductive view of women as mere temptresses. Accordingly the image of the woman in the water, her fair human half above the waves and her fish or serpent tail below, became a dangerous symbol of combined conscious and unconscious desires. She was thought to lack a soul and to use her power to lure men into the sea and drown them in order to steal their souls. She thus came to represent temptation and sin.

Dahut and the unconscious

In this story the image of the perilous mermaid is powerfully reflected in the person of Dahut, who also represents the old religion. While her father is still pagan, the two of them live in harmony and Dahut thrives. But after he has encountered Corentin and converted to the new religion, she begins to sicken. She explains that her illness is caused by the lack of joy or laughter. In other words, emotion and spontaneity have become suppressed. It is to remedy this imbalance that Dahut asks Gradlon to build her Ys. Being poised above the water, in Jungian terms Ys is allied with the feminine symbol of the unconscious. Because the new religion inclines towards the cerebral qualities of rationality and the rule of law, the instinctual and emotional aspects of the psyche have become neglected. This is why Dahut sickens. It is interesting that, after Gradlon builds the city, he decides to live there with his daughter. This shows that either he is vacillating between the two religions or that he, too, is aware of an imbalance.

Hermits

The figure of the hermit is important because it is a transitional one. Hermits were the lone clerics of Celtic Christianity. In Arthurian legend they appeared as healers and spiritual advisers to the knights. Being solitary they had a certain independence and were not much controlled by the hierarchy of the Church. Because they lived close to nature they represented a meeting point between the old druid and the new priest.

When Gradlon first meets Corentin, he is a hermit of the woods. The miraculous fish which is made whole again when returned to the well, is reminiscent of the ancient Salmon of Wisdom whose power was revered by the druids. In the figure of Corentin, therefore, we can see the transition from druid of the old religion, through the hermit of Celtic Christianity to the bishop of the Roman Catholic Church. The role of the hermit was also taken over by the Celtic saints whose wonders and miracles, especially in regard to animals, were clearly relics of original druidic and shamanic powers.

Dragons

The dragon, prevalent in Arthurian legend and Breton saints' tales, was an enlarged serpent and therefore symbolized the old matriarchal powers blown up to fearful proportions. Breton saints such as Gildas and Efflam distinguished themselves by taming dragons and then taking them to the clifftops where the beasts were obliged to drown themselves in the sea, thereby returning to the unconscious.

The nine druidesses

When Dahut goes to the druidic sisterhood on the Isle of Sein (sometimes known as the Fortunate Isles) she is visiting her own kind. The nine women have retreated to a lonely outpost where no man dare go. Their ancient regenerative powers are shown by their receiving the souls of the dead. Their number symbolizes their strong magic, being a tripling of the usual Celtic triplicity. They are linked to other supernatural groups of women in Celtic mythology, such as the nine sorceresses who guard the pearl-rimmed cauldron in the Celtic poem *Preiddeu Annwn*, the nine warrior witches in the tale of 'Peredur' and the company of queens who bear the dying Arthur away in a barge, chief of whom is Morgan le Fay. Breton water spirits were often called Morgan, *mor* being the Celtic word for 'sea'. Morgan le Fay, herself, was therefore a type of water goddess, perhaps the dark aspect of Nimue, the Lady of the Lake. The druidesses, as representatives of the old religion, are still in touch with elemental spirits, as symbolized by the Korrigans. But their ancient power is clearly under threat.

Flooding

Flooding symbolizes the forces of the unconscious overwhelming the conscious or the irrational overcoming the rational. The city of Ys has become corrupt, having overbalanced towards the instinctive aspects of the psyche. This overbalance leads to its destruction. Ys therefore drowns in its own excesses, the life-giving water rising up to become a watery grave. The image of flooding also denotes purification and the sweeping away of an old order. In this case the old pagan faith is being swept away by the new forces of Christianity.

The betrayer of the city is Dahut's red-robed lover, who is a type of the Christian devil. Because he awakens an overwhelming sexuality in Dahut at the same time as unlocking the sluice-gate, the deluge that follows also symbolizes the danger of excessive sexual desire.

Drowned islands

The motif of the drowned island is a pervasive one in ancient Celtic literature. It is commonly shown as a type of Celtic Otherworld to which men are lured by fairy women and where the Well of Wisdom can be found. Tales of such islands may have originated with the story of Atlantis that some say was inhabited by druids. When some of these turned to the black arts, the island was finally overwhelmed by the natural forces they had inadvertently conjured.

Negative anima

Like the goddess who has both light and dark faces (see pages 74–5), the anima, or internal female archetype, has been identified by Jung as having positive and negative aspects. When the realm of the feminine is attacked or disregarded, the dark side of the goddess can become split off from the light side. In psychological terms, the negative anima presents itself. She is the monstrous destroyer, the evil witch, the betraying lover or neglecting mother. She is also the *femme fatale*, who personifies dangerous and destructive illusion, leading to death.

In the story, Dahut becomes a black-hearted murderess after she has been usurped by Corentin. The killing of her lovers reflects her ancient role of regenerative nature goddess, as does her sexual appetite. But because the regenerative principle of the goddess is no longer acknowledged, she is now only the bringer of death.

Within the psyche, an imperfect relationship with the inner feminine, or a denigration of her, inevitably gives rise to the negative animus. Conversely, if the inner female figure is honoured, she becomes the key to the deepest riches of the soul. (For positive anima, see pages 48–9.)

14 | CONCLUSION

In Celtic myths we have seen much that is in the myths of other cultures and comes from a common pool of human experience; in fact the only theme strangely absent in the Celtic tradition is that of how the universe came into being. Yet Celtic myths treat the familiar themes in their own particular way, as well as having a number of special features of their own.

Gods into mortals

One factor that is particularly Celtic, as we have seen, is euhemerization: the transformation of gods into human figures. The euhemerization of gods such as the Dagda, Lugh and the Morrigan is relatively slight. Their powers are clearly divine and they are similar in many ways to the gods of other pantheons. Yet they are made human in so far as they are not quite omnipotent: like the Norse gods they are vulnerable – more so than the Greek gods; thus the Morrigan can be temporarily defeated by the mortal Cuchulainn. Unlike the Norse gods, however, these clearly divine Celtic gods do not actually die.

A far more euhemerized example is the Trickster Gwydion. The myth presents him as human, but a comparison with the Norse Odin (Germanic Woden), to whom his name may be related, underlines his divinity. Like Odin he is a consummate shape-shifter and gets his way by magic, cleverness and trickery rather than force. Gwydion is also adept in using magical verses; Odin has stolen the 'mead of the poets' from the giants. Gwydion stands at the foot of a tree and charms Lleu down with his verses; Odin has drunk from the fountain of knowledge at the foot of the World Tree, Yggdrasil.

Heroes

Probably the most widespread mythical archetype is the hero. The myths we have looked at present a range of heroic variations, from the powerfully destructive, to the subtle, the self-denying and the self-sacrificing.

In Cuchulainn we have an old-style epic hero, like the Babylonian Gilgamesh. In setting out on his first journey to Emain he resembles Theseus; both set out to prove themselves by going in search of a father or father-figure. When Cuchulainn is sent on the dangerous mission to seek training with Scathach, he is like Perseus, sent to fetch the head of Medusa. In some ways Cuchulainn is like Shiva, terrible in his powers of destruction, or like the Norse Thor, who wields power through his thunder hammer. Cuchulainn is described in the *Tain* as performing 'thunder feats' and his magical weapon the *gaibolga* resembles Thor's hammer.

Lleu is a different kind of hero. He achieves no great feats, apart from the symbolic one of killing the 'old king' in the guise of the wren, but he is another euhemerized god – closely related in derivation to Lugh, the multi-skilled god of light, and he shares several features with other heroes. He begins life as an indeterminate 'something', like Native American heroes who enter the world as shapeless blood-clots. He is of doubtful paternity – resembling, for example, Perseus, Oedipus and many Native American heroes; he starts life in a wooden chest, like Perseus (and also with echoes of the Egyptian Osiris); he passes symbolic tests, or initiations, set by Arianrhod; and though bearing a charmed life he is killed through trickery, yet resurrected – like the Norse gods Odin (who also hangs on a tree) and Baldur (also a son of light), Attis, and other god-heroes, including Christ.

Goddesses

We have also seen strong heroines representing goddesses. Deirdre and Grainne both assert their right to marry the husband-consort of their choice and yet must battle with the forces of patriarchy in the shape of elderly male authority figures, Conchobor and Finn. In both these cases the natural order is usurped when the young man is killed. As we have seen, there is also a seasonal aspect to this, since the Celtic heroine-goddess represents the land, which must be fertilized by the dying of winter (old king) and the onset of spring and summer (new king).

In Goewin and Arianrhod we have aspects of the virgin goddess, the latter representing what happens when the Goddess is disrespected – although Arianrhod also 'sets tests' for Lleu. Medb is another powerful female figure, spurred to action by the challenge of a threat to the power of the feminine. Celtic myth is particularly rich in these powerful goddess figures, who are equal to those in other cultures, such as Pallas Athene, Ishtar, Kali and the White Buffalo Woman of the Lakota Sioux. Dahut is another goddess figure, although, through the filter of the new religion of Christianity, she is seen as negative anima: overwhelmed by the power of the unconscious which she herself represents.

Love triangles

An interesting feature of Celtic myths is the prevalence of love triangles. We have, for example: Deirdre–Naoise–Conchobor, Grainne–Diarmuid–Finn, Blodeuwedd–Lleu–Gronwy and Iseult–Tristan–Mark – who foreshadow the famous triangle of Guinevere, Lancelot and Arthur. There is a hint of the love triangle in the relationship between Pwll, Arawn and the Queen, although more typical is an episode later in the branch when Pwll wins Rhiannon from Gwawl. These triangles are linked to the seasonal theme discussed earlier, as well as to the general Celtic attraction to triplicity – the 'power of three'. Part of the appeal may lie in the way in which the number three represents thesis, antithesis and synthesis, or resolution. Seen from a more Freudian angle it represents the two parents with the addition of the child.

The Otherworld

Although most myth systems have some form of afterlife or Land of the Dead, Celtic culture is probably unique in its concept of the Otherworld. An essential part of this is the absence of sin and guilt in the Celtic world view. Hence, as we have seen, for the Celts the Otherworld is not divided into heaven and hell. It is something like the Christian heaven, or the Greek elysium, but unlike these it is not restricted to the heroic or virtuous. It is also unusual in that its human occupants eventually reincarnate into this world.

In the story of Oisin's journey to the Otherworld we see a possibly shamanistic journey into a realm of the unconscious, with a corresponding alteration of perceived time. The fairy woman Niamh is another goddess, or at least an anima figure. Her riding on the water echoes Odin's ability to do the same, as well as Christ's walking on the Sea of Galilee. The more euhemerized story of Pwll also involves a stay in the Otherworld, or Underworld, and in 'Finn and the Salmon of Wisdom' the young hero taps into Otherworldly wisdom.

One feature that the Otherworld shares with depictions of spirit worlds in the myths of other cultures is that of crossing or entering water to get there, as we have seen in the story of Oisin. This also happens, for example, in a Blackfoot Indian myth in which the hero dives into a lake to find another world from which he brings back horses for his tribe. Another shared feature is the idea of being led into the Otherworld or spirit world by an animal, perhaps symbolizing a more instinctive aspect of the self.

'The Voyage of Maeldun', meanwhile, is Otherworldly in a different sense. Maeldun's journey resembles other sea quests (such as that of Odysseus and Jason) and quest myths worldwide. It is a journey to, or through, the Otherworld, but perhaps one taken by the soul after death. It shows the power of myth to adapt and embrace new circumstances, in that the final reward of this journey, at least in the surviving version of the tale, is enlightenment in the form of Christian forgiveness, rather than the revenge that Maeldun has set out to achieve. In the story of Ys, by way of contrast, the Christian influence ensures that the Otherworld city is inundated, lost for ever beneath the waves of the unconscious.

SELECT BIBLIOGRAPHY AND DISCOGRAPHY

Books

Ammianus Marcellinus (trans. John C. Rolfe), Heinemann, 1950

Aubert, O.-L. Aubert, *Celtic Legends of Brittany*, Coop Breizh (Kerangwenn), 1993

Boa, Frazer, *The Way of Myth: Talking with Joseph Campbell*, Shambhala, 1994

Baring, Anne, and Cashford, Jules, *The Myth of the Goddess*, Penguin, 1993

Caesar (trans. S. A. Handford), *The Conquest of Gaul*, Penguin, 1982

Campbell, John F., *Popular Tales of the West Highlands*, Birlinn, 1994

Campbell, Joseph, *The Hero with a Thousand Faces*, Fontana, 1993

— *The Power of Myth*, Doubleday, 1991

Cross, T. P. and Slover, C. H., *Ancient Irish Tales*, Figgis (Dublin), 1936

Cunliffe, Barry, *The Ancient Celts*, Oxford University Press, 1997

Delaney, Frank, *Legends of the Celts*, HarperCollins, 1994

Diodorus Siculus (trans. C. H. Oldfather), *Historical Library*, 1933

Duncan, Anthony, *The Elements of Celtic Christianity*, Element Books, 1992

Eddy, Steve and Hamilton, Claire, *Timeless Wisdom of the Celts*, Hodder & Stoughton, 1999

Ellis, Peter Berresford, *The Druids*, Constable, 1994
    Caesar's Invasion of Britain, Constable, 1994

Gantz, Jeffrey (trans.), *The Mabinogion*, Penguin, 1976

Green, Miranda, *Celtic Myths*, British Museum Press, 1993

Hope, Murray, *The Ancient Wisdom of the Celts*, Thorsons, 1995

Hyde, Douglas, *A Literary History of Ireland*, T. Fisher Unwin, 1899

Jackson, Kenneth Hurlstone (trans.), *A Celtic Miscellany*, Penguin, 1971

Joyce, P. W., *Old Celtic Romances*, Longman, 1920

Jung, C. G. *The Archetypes and the Collective Unconscious*, Routledge, 1959
— *Man and his Symbols*, Penguin 1964

Kinsella, Thomas, (trans.), *The Tain*, Oxford University Press, 1990
— *The New Oxford Book of Irish Verse*, Oxford University Press, 1992

Laing, Lloyd and Jennifer, *Art of the Celts,* Thames & Hudson, 1992

MacCulloch, J. A., *The Religion of the Ancient Celts*, Constable, 1991

Matthews, Caitlín, *Mabon and the Mysteries of Britain*, Arkana, 1987
— *The Celtic Tradition*, Element, 1989

Matthews, Caitlín and John, *The Encyclopaedia of Celtic Wisdom*, Element, 1994

Matthews, John, *Taliesin,* Aquarian Press, 1991

Pearson, Carol S., *Awakening the Heroes Within*, HarperCollins, 1991

Rolleston, T. W., *Celtic Myths and Legends*, Senate, 1994

Rutherford, Ward, *Celtic Mythology,* Thorsons, 1995

Stewart, R. J., *Celtic Gods Celtic Goddesses,* Blandford, 1997

Strabo (trans. H. L. Jones), *Geography*, Heinemann, 1917

Tacitus (trans. Michael Grant), *The Annals of Imperial Rome*, Penguin, 1971

Zaczek, Iain, *Chronicles of the Celts*, Collins & Brown, 1996

Recorded discussion

Campbell, Joseph with Moyers, Bill, *The Power of Myth* (six audio-cassettes), High Bridge with *Parabola* Magazine

Music

Noirin Ni Riain, *Celtic Soul*, Earth Music Productions,
  LMUS 0031
Loreena McKennitt, *Parallel Dreams*, Quinlan Road Ltd, Canada,
  QRCD 103
Celtic Woman (compilation), Celtic Woman Records,
  CWRCD 7001
Alan Stivell, *Renaissance of the Celtic Harp*, Rounder Records,
  Massachusetts, CD 3067

Other material

Available from C. Hamilton c/o the publisher, or at
  Claire@hamiltonharps.freeserve.co.uk

Company of Strangers, *Blodeuwedd – A Wife out of Flowers*,
  COS 298
Company of Strangers, *The Love Song of Diarmuid and Grainne*,
  CSSM1 (cassette)
The Celtic Harp, Sound and Media Ltd, SUMCD 4133
The Celtic Harp Collection, Claire Hamilton, e2 ETD CD/003
Celtic Myths, Claire Hamilton (harp and spoken word), Music
  Collection International ETD CD/157

INDEX

Other related titles

TEACH YOURSELF

GREEK MYTHS

Steve Eddy & Claire Hamilton

Myths are symbolic stories that have evolved through oral tradition, and they have guided and inspired us for many years. Follow these lively retellings of popular and significant Greek myths and discover how to unlock their hidden meanings so that they can be better understood.

- Explore and enjoy the subtle truths these tales have to offer.
- Discover more about the heritage of Greek mythology.
- Bring these ancient myths to life by discovering how to interpret them.
- Place Greek myths in a cultural and global context.

Steve Eddy is a former English teacher and author of several books on esoteric subjects. Claire Hamilton is a writer, performer and Celtic harpist. She has explored myths in all these capacities and has an MA in The Bardic Tradition in Ireland.